W9-BTS-949

The Tempest

By William Shakespeare

Prestwick House
Literary Touchstone Classics™

P.O. Box 658 • Clayton, Delaware 19938

Senior Editor: Paul Moliken

Editors: Lisa M. Miller and Mary Grimes

Cover Design: Kyle Price

Production: Jerry Clark

Prestwick House
Literary Touchstone Classics
P.O. Box 658 • Clayton, Delaware 19938
Tel: 1.800.932.4593
Fax: 1.888.718.9333
Web: www.prestwickhouse.com

Prestwick House Teaching Units™, Activity Packs™, and Response Journals™ are the perfect complement for these editions. To purchase teaching resources for this book, visit www.prestwickhouse.com/material

ISBN-10: 1-58049-337-8
ISBN-13: 978-1-58049-337-6

Contents

Strategies for Understanding Shakespeare's Language

1. **When reading verse, note the appropriate phrasing and intonation.**

   DO NOT PAUSE AT THE END OF A LINE unless there is a mark of punctuation. Shakespearean verse has a rhythm of its own, and once a reader gets used to it, the rhythm becomes very natural to speak in and read. Beginning readers often find it helpful to read a short pause at a comma and a long pause for a period, colon, semicolon, dash, or question mark.

Here's an example from *The Merchant of Venice*, Act IV, Scene i:

The quality of mercy is not strain'd, *(short pause)*
It droppeth as the gentle rain from heaven
Upon the place beneath: *(long pause)* it is twice blest; *(long pause)*
It blesseth him that gives, *(short pause)* and him that takes; *(long pause)*
'Tis mightiest in the mighties; *(long pause)* it becomes
The throned monarch better than his crown; *(long pause)*

2. **Reading from punctuation mark to punctuation mark for meaning.**

   In addition to helping you read aloud, punctuation marks define units of thought. Try to understand each unit as you read, keeping in mind that periods, colons, semicolons, and question marks signal the end of a thought. Here's an example from ***The Taming of the Shrew***:

   LUC. Tranio, I saw her coral lips to move,
   And with her breath she did perfume the air;
   Sacred, and sweet, was all I saw in her.
   TRA. Nay, then, 't is time to stir him from his
   trance.
   I pray, awake, sir: if you love the maid,
   Bend thoughts and wits to achieve her. (I,i)

   The first unit of thought is from "Tranio" to "air":
   He saw her lips move, and her breath perfumed the air.

The second thought ("Sacred, and sweet...") re-emphasizes the first.

   Tranio replies that Lucentio needs to awaken from his trance and try to win "the maid." These two sentences can be considered one unit of thought.

3. In an **inverted sentence**, the verb comes before the subject. Some lines will be easier to understand if you put the subject first and reword the sentence. For example, look at the line below:

"Never was seen so black a day as this:" (Romeo and Juliet, IV, v)

You can change its inverted pattern so it is more easily understood:

"A day as black as this was never seen:"

4. An **ellipsis** occurs when a word or phrase is left out. In *Romeo and Juliet,* Benvolio asks Romeo's father and mother if they know the problem that is bothering their son. Romeo's father answers:

   "I neither know **it** *nor can learn of* **him***" (Romeo and Juliet I,i).*

   This sentence can easily be understood to mean,

   "I neither know [the cause of] it,
   nor can [I] learn [about it from] him."

5. As you read longer speeches, keep track of the subject, verb, and object – *who* did *what* to *whom.*

   In the clauses below, note the subject, verbs, and objects.

   ROSS: The king hath happily received, Macbeth,
   The news of thy success: and when he reads
   Thy personal venture in the rebel's fight... (*Macbeth* I, iii)

   1st clause: *The king hath happily received, Macbeth,/The news of thy success:*
   SUBJECT – The king
   VERB – has received
   OBJECT – the news [of Macbeth's success]
   2nd clause: *and when he reads/thy personal venture in the rebel's fight,*

   SUBJECT – he [the king]
   VERB – reads
   OBJECT – [about] your venture

   In addition to following the subject, verb, and object of a clause, you also need to track pronoun references. In the following soliloquy Romeo, who is madly in love with Juliet, secretly observes her as she steps out on her balcony. To help you keep track of the pronoun references, we've made margin notes. (Note that the feminine pronoun sometimes refers to Juliet, but sometimes does not.)
   But, soft! what light through yonder window breaks?
   It is the east, and Juliet is the sun!
   Arise, fair sun, and kill the envious moon,

Who* is already sick and pale with grief, *"Who" refers to the moon.*
That thou her* maid art more fair than she:* *"thou her maid" refers to Juliet, the sun.*
"she" and "her" refer to the moon.

In tracking the line of action in a passage, it is useful to identify the main thoughts that are being expressed and paraphrase them. Note the following passage in which Hamlet expresses his feelings about the death of his father and the remarriage of his mother:

O God! a beast that wants discourse of reason
Would have mourn'd longer – married with my uncle,
My father's brother, but no more like my father
Than I to Hercules. (I,ii)

Paraphrasing the three main points, we find that Hamlet is saying:

- a mindless beast would have mourned the death of its mate longer than my mother did
- she married my uncle, my father's brother
- my uncle is not at all like my father

If you are having trouble understanding Shakespeare, the first rule is to read it out loud, just as an actor rehearsing would have to do. That will help you understand how one thought is connected to another.

6. Shakespeare frequently uses metaphor to illustrate an idea in a unique way. Pay careful attention to the two dissimilar objects or ideas being compared. In *Macbeth*, Duncan, the king says:

   I have begun to plant thee, and will labour
   To make thee full of growing. (I,v)

   The king compares Macbeth to a tree he can plant and watch grow.

7. An *allusion* is a reference to some event, person, place, or artistic work, not directly explained or discussed by the writer; it relies on the reader's familiarity with the item referred to. Allusion is a quick way of conveying information or presenting an image. In the following lines, Romeo alludes to Diana, goddess of the hunt and of chastity, and to Cupid's arrow (love).

   ROMEO: Well, in that hit you miss: she'll not be hit
   with Cupid's arrow, she hath Dian's wit;
   and in strong proof of chastity well arm'd (I,i)

8. Contracted words are words in which a letter has been left out. Some that frequently appear:

be't	on't	wi'
do't	t'	'sblood
'gainst	ta'en	i'
'tis	e'en	
'bout	know'st	'twill
ne'er	o'	o'er

9. Archaic, obsolete and familiar words with unfamiliar definitions may also cause problems.

   - **Archaic Words** Some archaic words, like *thee, thou, thy*, and *thine,* are instantly understandable, while others, like *betwixt,* cause a momentary pause.
   - **Obsolete Words** If it were not for the notes in a Shakespeare text, obsolete words could be a problem; words like "beteem" are usually not found in student dictionaries. In these situations, however, a quick glance at the book's notes will solve the problem.
   - **Familiar Words with Unfamiliar Definitions** Another problem is those familiar words whose definitions have changed. Because readers think they know the word, they do not check the notes. For example, in this comment from *Much Ado About Nothing*, the word *an* means *if*:

     Beatrice: Scratching could not make it worse, *an* 'twere such a face as yours were. (I,i)

     For this kind of word, we have included margin notes.

10. Wordplay: puns, double entendres, and malapropisms

    - A *pun* is a literary device that achieves humor or emphasis by playing on ambiguities. Two distinct meanings are suggested either by the same word or by two similar-sounding words.
    - A *double entendre* is a kind of pun in which a word or phrase has a second, usually sexual, meaning.
    - A *malapropism* occurs when a character mistakenly uses a word that he or she has confused with another word. In *Romeo and Juliet,* the Nurse tells Romeo that she needs to have a "confidence" with him, when she should have said "conference." Mockingly, Benvolio then says she probably will "indite" (rather than "invite") Romeo to dinner.

Reading Pointers for Sharper Insights

Consider the following as you read *The Tempest:*

1. **Prospero's magic**: Prospero's magic is obviously the cause of his downfall. His motive is flawed because he longs for knowledge that mankind fears and considers evil and dangerous. On the island, however, his magic symbolizes his overall power, which shows the audience that he was most likely a strong leader when he was duke. Prospero's magic is the basis for this play; the play could not exist without it. Now that his dukedom has been taken from him the only strength he has is his magical ability, and it is through his magic that Prospero is finally able to get revenge.

2. **The Tempest**: The storm Prospero creates sets the tone for the entire play. The tumultuous weather serves as a motif for the suffering Prospero has endured. Being forced into exile by his brother and living on an island with his daughter has caused Prospero much grief and sorrow. His exile has caused him to grow angry, and now he wants revenge.

3. **Appearance versus Reality**: Once the men shipwreck on Prospero's island, they are immediately exposed to more magic. Throughout the play, appearances are altered, not only through magic, but also through role reversals and class distinctions (see ***Class Distinctions*** below). Shakespeare's use of appearance versus reality is a common technique he uses in many of his plays, especially in reference to the use of magic. There are several instances in which Prospero conjures spirits who take on appearances of gods or goddesses. In addition, one particular spirit imitates the voice of other characters to cause conflict between the characters. These magical interventions confuse reality and make things appear completely different from what they really are.

4. **Miranda's character**: Miranda is Prospero's daughter, and she knows nothing other than life on the island. Although she does not play a major role, Shakespeare does make her an unforgettable character, simply because of her unconventional behavior. Miranda proves that she is not a typical female, especially in her argument with Caliban. She has no female role model to show her the way a woman should act; however, she is still proper and respectful to her father. The portrayal of Miranda's character shows Shakespeare's insight and his awareness that a person's environment shapes his or her personality.

5. **Class Distinction:** Throughout the play it is obvious who ranks higher in social status. First, class distinction can be noticed through the character's speech. Typically, if the character is of low social status, he or she will speak in prose, and if he or she is of higher rank, the lines will be written in verse. With the use of magic, Prospero confuses these distinctions. When Stephano and Trinculo meet Caliban, Stephano immediately takes charge as leader, and later refers to himself as king of the island. In addition, Ferdinand, Prince of Milan, is treated as a servant by Prospero, which Ferdinand readily accepts in the name of love. Note the changes in class distinctions as the play progresses.

6. **Dreams:** Whenever Prospero inflicts characters with his magic they associate their experience with dreams. This is another technique Shakespeare has used in several of his plays. Shakespeare's audience would have been vehemently opposed to the use of magic. Because the characters believe they are dreaming, the magic is not a threatening element of the play. Incorporating magic in such a way helps make Prospero's magic acceptable to a fearful audience.

7. **Redemption:** Despite his use of magic, Prospero is a sympathetic and likable character because he admits that learning sorcery is evil. From the beginning, there are hints and inclinations that Prospero desires to repent, which contrasts with King Alonso and the Duke of Milan, Antonio. King Alonso and Antonio do not long for redemption until they learn who caused the tempest—up until that point, they are unrepentant.

BY WILLIAM SHAKESPEARE

DRAMATIS PERSONÆ

ALONSO, King of Naples
FERDINAND, son to the King of Naples
SEBASTIAN, his brother
PROSPERO, the rightful Duke of Milan
ANTONIO, his brother, the usurping Duke of Milan
GONZALO, an honest old counsellor
ADRIAN and FRANCISCO, lords
STEPHANO, Alonso's drunken butler
TRINCULO, a jester
MASTER of a ship
BOATSWAIN
MARINERS
CALIBAN, a savage and deformed slave
MIRANDA, his daughter
ARIEL, an airy spirit and Prospero's attendant
IRIS
CERES
JUNO
NYMYPHS
REAPERS } spirits

SCENE: *On a ship at sea; afterwards on an uninhabited island.*

THE TEMPEST

ACT I

SCENE I

On a ship at sea. A tempestuous noise of thunder and lightning heard.

[Enter a Master and a Boatswain]

MASTER: Boatswain!

BOATS: Here, Master. What cheer?

MASTER: Good,[1] speak to the mariners. Fall to't, yarely,[2] or we run ourselves aground. Bestir[3] *Exit*

Enter Mariners

BOATS: Heigh, my hearts![4] Cheerly, cheerly, my hearts! Yare, yare! Take in the topsail.† Tend[5] to the Master's whistle! Blow, till thou burst thy wind, if room enough!†

[1] *'Good, you're here.'*

[2] *right away, quickly*

[3] *'get up,' 'arise'*

[4] *hearties; mates*

[5] *Listen; Pay attention*

[Enter Alonso, Sebastian, Antonio, Ferdinand, Gonzalo, and others]

ALONSO: Good Boatswain, have care. Where's the Master? [*To the Mariners*] Play the men![6]

BOATS: I pray now, keep below.

ANTONIO: Where is the Master, Boatswain?

BOATS: Do you not hear him? You mar our labour. Keep your cabins: you do assist the storm.

GONZ: Nay, good,[7] be patient.

BOATS: When the sea is. Hence! What cares these roarers for the name of the king?† To cabin: silence! Trouble us not.

GONZ: Good, yet remember whom thou has aboard.

BOATS: None that I more love than myself. You are a counsellor;† if you can command these elements to silence, and work

[6] *'Act like men!'*

[7] *'Good man'*

†Terms marked in the text with (†) can be looked up in the Glossary for additional information.

the peace of the present, we will not hand[8] a rope more; use your authority. If you cannot, give thanks you have lived so long, and make yourself ready in your cabin for the mischance of the hour, if it so hap. [*To the Mariners*] Cheerly, good hearts! [*To Gonzalo*] Out of our way, I say! *Exit*

GONZ: I have great comfort from this fellow. Methinks he hath no drowning mark upon him; his complexion is perfect gallows.† Stand fast, good Fate, to his hanging. Make the rope of his destiny our cable, for our own doth little advantage.†[9] If he be not born to be hanged, our case is miserable. *Exeunt*

[*Enter Boatswain*]

BOATS: Down with the topmast!† Yare! Lower, lower! Bring her to try with main-course!† [*A cry within*] A plague upon this howling! They[10] are louder than the weather or our office.[11]

[*Enter Sebastian, Antonio, and Gonzalo*]

Yet again! What do you here? Shall we give o'er[12] and drown? Have you a mind to sink?

SEBAST: A pox o' your throat, you bawling, blasphemous, incharitable dog!

BOATS: Work you, then.

ANTONIO: Hang, cur,[13] hang, you whoreson, insolent noise-maker! We are less afraid to be drowned than thou art.

GONZ: I'll warrant him for drowning,† though[14] the ship were no stronger than a nutshell and as leaky as an unstanched[15] wench.

BOATS: Lay her a-hold, a-hold! Set her two courses!† Off to sea again; lay her off!†

[*Enter Mariners wet*]

MARINERS: All lost! To prayers, to prayers! All lost! [*Exeunt Mariners*]

BOATS: What, must our mouths be cold?†

GONZ: The king and prince at prayers! Let's assist them,
For our case is theirs.

SEBAST: I'm out of patience.

[8] *handle*

[9] *has little use*

[10] *the other passengers*

[11] *work*

[12] *up; over (to the weather)*

[13] *coward; dog*

[14] *even if*

[15] *freely flowing*

ANTONIO: We are merely[16] cheated of our lives by drunkards.
This wide-chopped[17] rascal—would thou mightst lie drowning
The washing of ten tides![†]

GONZ: He'll be hanged yet,
Though every drop of water swear against it,
And gape at wid'st to glut[18] him.

[A confused noise within]

MARINERS: 'Mercy on us!'—'We split, we split!'—'Farewell, my wife and children!'—'Farewell, brother!'—'We split, we split, we split!' *[Exit Boatswain]*

ANTONIO: Let's all sink wi'th' King.

SEBAST: Let's take leave of him. *[Exeunt Antonio and Sebastian]*

GONZ: Now would I give a thousand furlongs of sea for an acre of barren ground—long heath, brown furze, anything.[†] The wills above be done, but I would fain die a dry death.

[Exeunt]

[16]*completely; utterly*

[17]*big mouthed*

[18]*widest so as to swallow*

SCENE II

The Island. Before Prospero's cell.

[Enter Prospero and Miranda]

MIRAN: If by your art,[1] my dearest father, you have
Put the wild waters in this roar, allay them.
The sky, it seems, would pour down stinking pitch,[†]
But that the sea, mounting to th' welkin's[2] cheek,
Dashes the fire out. O, I have suffered
With those that I saw suffer! A brave[3] vessel,
Who had, no doubt, some noble creature in her,
Dashed all to pieces! O, the cry did knock
Against my very heart! Poor souls, the perished.
Had I been any god of power, I would
Have sunk the sea within the earth, or ere[4]
It should the good ship so have swallowed and
The fraughting souls[5] within her.

PROSP: Be collected.
No more amazement.[6] Tell your piteous[7] heart
There's no harm done.

MIRAN: O, woe the day!

[1]*magic powers*

[2]*sky's*

[3]*splendid; noble*

[4]*before*

[5]*difficulty of storing the cargo*

[6]*overwhelming fear, horror*

[7]*pitying*

Prosp: No harm.
I have done nothing but in care of thee,
Of thee, my dear one, thee, my daughter, who
Art ignorant of what thou art, naught knowing
Of whence I am, nor that I am more better[8]
Than Prospero, master of a full poor cell,
And thy no greater father.
Miran: More to know
Did never meddle with[9] my thoughts.
Prosp: 'Tis time
I should inform thee farther. Lend thy hand,
And pluck my magic garment from me.—So:
[Lays down his cloak]
Lie there, my art.—Wipe thou thine eyes; have comfort.
The direful spectacle of the wreck, which touched
The very virtue of compassion in thee,
I have with such provision[10] in mine art
So safely ordered that there is no soul—
No, not so much perdition[11] as an hair
Betid[12] to any creature in the vessel
Which[13] thou heard'st cry, which though saw'st sink. Sit down;
For thou must now know farther.
[Miranda sits]
Miran: You have often
Begun to tell me what I am, but stopped
And left me to a bootless inquisition,[14]
Concluding 'Stay, not yet.'
Prosp: The hour's now come;
The very minute bids thee ope[15] thine ear,
Obey, and be attentive. Canst thou remember
A time before we came unto this cell?
I do not think thou canst, for then thou wast not
Out[16] three years old.
Miran: Certainly, sir, I can.
Prosp: By what? By any other house or person?
Of anything the image tell me[17] that
Hath kept with thy remembrance.
Miran: 'Tis far off,
And rather like a dream than an assurance[18]
That my remembrance warrants.[19] Had I not
Four or five women once that tended me?

[8] *of a higher rank (socially)*
[9] *interfere upon*
[10] *caution; foresight*
[11] *loss; horror*
[12] *Happened*
[13] *Whom*
[14] *profitless search*
[15] *open*
[16] *Fully; Beyond*
[17] *Describe whatever the memory*
[18] *truth*
[19] *guarantees as a truth*

PROSP: Thou hadst, and more, Miranda. But how is it
That this lives in thy mind? What seest thou else
In the dark backward[20] and abyss of time?
If thou rememb'rest aught[21] ere thou cam'st here,
How thou cam'st here thou mayst.

MIRAN: But that I do not.

PROSP: Twelve year since, Miranda, twelve year since,
Thy father was the Duke of Milan, and
A prince of power—

MIRAN: Sir, are not you my father?

PROSP: Thy mother was a piece[22] of virtue, and
She said thou wast my daughter; and thy father
Was Duke of Milan, and his only heir
And princess no worse issued.[23]

MIRAN: O, the heavens!
What foul play had we that we came from thence?
Or blessèd† was't we did?

PROSP: Both, both, my girl.
By foul play, as thou sayst, were we heaved thence,
But blessedly holp[24] hither.

MIRAN: O, my heart bleeds
To think o'th' teen[25] that I have turned you to,
Which is from[26] my remembrance. Please you, farther.

PROSP: My brother and thy uncle, called Antonio—
I pray thee mark me, that a brother should
Be so perfidious—he whom next[27] thyself
Of all the world I loved, and to him put
The manage[28] of my state; as at that time
Through all the signories[29] it was the first,
And Prospero the prime duke, being so reputed
In dignity, and for the liberal arts[30]
Without a parallel; those being all my study,
The government I cast upon my brother,
And to my state grew stranger, being transported
And rapt† in secret studies. Thy false uncle—
Dost thou attend me?

MIRAN: Sir, most heedfully.

PROSP: Being once perfected how to grant suits,[31]
How to deny them, who t'advance and who
To trash[32] for over-topping,[33] new created
The creatures[34]† that were mine, I say, or changed 'em,
Or else new formed 'em;† having both the key[35]

[20] *past*

[21] *anything*

[22] *a perfect representation*

[23] *no less a descendant of nobility*

[24] *helped*

[25] *hardship; heartache, grief*

[26] *away from*

[27] *after, following*

[28] *management, control*

[29] *areas*

[30] *improvement of the mind*

[31] *Having become skilled in handling suitors*

[32] *to restrain*

[33] *attaining too much power or authority*

[34] *dependents*

[35] *control, power*

Of officer and office, set all hearts i'th' state
To what tune† pleased his ear, that[36] now he was
The ivy which had hid my princely trunk,
And sucked my verdure out on't. Thou attend'st not!

Miran: O good sir, I do.

Prosp: I pray thee mark me.
I, thus neglecting worldly ends, all dedicated
To closeness[37] and the bettering of my mind
With that which, but[38] by being so retired,[39]
O'er prized all popular rate,[40] in my false brother
Awakened an evil nature; and my trust,
Like a good parent,† did beget of him
A falsehood, in its contrary[41] as great
As my trust was, which had indeed no limit,
A confidence sans[42]bound. He being thus lorded,
Not only with what my revenue yielded,
But what my power might else exact, like one
Who having into[43] truth, by telling of it,
Made such a sinner of his memory
To[44] credit his own lie,† he did believe
He was indeed the duke; out o'th'[45] substitution,
And executing[46] the outward face[47] of royalty
With all prerogative;[48] hence his ambition growing—
Dost thou hear?

Miran: Your tale, sir, would cure deafness.

Prosp: To have no screen[49] between this part he played
And him he played it for;† he needs will be
Absolute Milan.[50] Me, poor man, my library
Was dukedom large enough: of temporal royalties[51]
He thinks me now incapable; confederates[52]—
So dry[53] he was for sway[54]—with the King of Naples
To give him annual tribute, do him homage,
Subject his[55] coronet to his[56] crown, and bend
The dukedom, yet unbowed alas, poor Milan!—
To most ignoble stooping.†

Miran: O the heavens!

Prosp: Mark his condition[57]and th'event;[58] then tell me
If this might be a brother.

Miran: I should sin
To think but nobly of my grandmother:
Good wombs have borne bad sons.†

Prosp: Now the condition.

[36] *so that*

[37] *solitude, isolation*

[38] *merely*

[39] *private*

[40] *Became too priceless for commoners' understanding*

[41] *negative, opposite, or uncharacteristic qualities*

[42] *without*

[43] *taking possession of*

[44] *So as to*

[45] *as a result of the*

[46] *portraying*

[47] *symbol, image*

[48] *rights, privileges*

[49] *barrier*

[50] *Perfect Duke of Milan*

[51] *rule*

[52] *forms a plot, conspires*

[53] *thirsty; eager*

[54] *power, control*

[55] *Antonio's*

[56] *Alonso, King of Naples*

[57] *agreement*

[58] *outcome*

The King of Naples, being an enemy
To me inveterate, hearkens[59] my brother's suit;
Which was that he, in lieu o'th' premises[60]
Of homage and I know not how much tribute,
Should presently extirpate[61] me and mine
Out of the dukedom, and confer fair Milan,
With all the honours, on my brother; whereon,
A treacherous army levied, one midnight
Fated to th' purpose did Antonio open
The gates of Milan, and, i'th' dead of darkness,
The ministers[62] for th' purpose hurried thence[63]
Me and thy crying self.

MIRAN: Alack, for pity!
I, not rememb'ring how I cried out then,
Will cry it o'er again: it is a hint[64]
That wrings mine eyes to't.

PROSP: Hear a little further,
And then I'll bring thee to the present business
Which now's upon's; without the which this story
Were most impertinent.[65]

MIRAN: Wherefore did they not
That hour destroy us?

PROSP: Well demanded, wench;[66]
My tale provokes that question. Dear, they durst not,
So dear the love my people bore me, nor set
A mark so bloody on the business, but
With colours fairer painted their foul ends
In few,[67] they hurried us aboard a barque,[68]
Bore us some leagues to sea, where they prepared
A rotten carcass of a butt,† not rigged,
Nor tackle, sail, nor mast—the very rats
Instinctively have quit it. There they hoist us,
To cry to th' sea that roared to us, to sigh
To th' winds, whose pity, sighing back again,
Did us but loving wrong.†

MIRAN: Alack, what trouble
Was I then to you!

PROSP: O, a cherubin[69]
Thou wast that did preserve me. Thou didst smile,
Infused with a fortitude from heaven,
When I have decked[70] the sea with drops full salt,
Under my burden groaned;† which raised in me

[59] *listens to*

[60] *in return for the agreed upon conditions*

[61] *uproot; destroy*

[62] *agents*

[63] *from there*

[64] *occasion*

[65] *irrelevant, unconnected*

[66] *a young woman*

[67] *shortly*

[68] *ship*

[69] *angel*

[70] *covered*

An undergoing stomach,[71] to bear up
Against what should ensue.

MIRAN: How came we ashore?

PROSP: By Providence divine.
Some food we had, and some fresh water, that
A noble Neapolitan, Gonzalo,
Out of his charity,—who being then appointed
Master of this design,—did give us; with
Rich garments, linens, stuffs, and necessaries,
Which since have steaded[72] much; so, of his
gentleness[73]
Knowing I loved my books, he furnished me
From mine own library with volumes that
I prize above my dukedom.

MIRAN: Would I might
But ever see that man!

PROSP: Now I arise.

[Standing, he puts on his cloak]

Sit still, and hear the last of our sea-sorrow.
Here in this island we arrived, and here
Have I, thy schoolmaster, made thee more profit[74]
Than other princesess' can, that have more time
For vainer hours and tutors not so careful.[75]

MIRAN: Heavens thank you for't. And now I pray you, sir—
For still 'tis beating in my mind,—your reason
For raising this sea-storm.

PROSP: Know thus far north.
By accident most strange, bountiful Fortune,[†]
Now my dear lady,[76] hath mine enemies
Brought to this shore; and by my prescience
I find my zenith doth depend upon
A most auspicious star,[†] whose influence
If now I court not, but omit,[77] my fortunes
Will ever after droop. Here cease more questions:
Thou art inclined to sleep; 'tis a good dulness,[78]
And give it way—I know thou canst not choose.

[Miranda sleeps]

Come away,[79] servant, come!
I am ready now.
Approach, my Ariel, come!

[Enter Ariel]

[71] *the courage to live on*

[72] *been helpful*

[73] *kindness and nobility*

[74] *benefit or profit more*

[75] *caring, kind*

[76] *Fortune (an appositive)*

[77] *ignore, disregard*

[78] *drowsiness*

[79] *here*

ARIEL: All hail, great master, grave sir, hail! I come
To answer thy best pleasure; be't to fly,
To swim, to dive into the fire, to ride
On the curled clouds, to thy strong bidding task
Ariel and all his quality.[80]

PROSP: Hast thou, spirit,
Performed[81] to point[82] the tempest that I bade thee?

ARIEL: To every article.
I boarded the King's ship; now on the beak,[83]
Now in the waist,[84] the deck, in every cabin,
I flamed amazement.[85] Sometime I'd divide,
And burn in many places;† on the topmast,
The yards and bowsprit, would I flame distinctly,[86]
Then meet and join. Jove's lightning,† the precursors
O'th' dreadful thunder-claps, more momentary
And sight-outrunning[87] were not; the fire and cracks
Of sulphurous† roaring the most mighty Neptune†
Seem to besiege and make his bold waves tremble,
Yea, his dread trident shake.

PROSP: My brave spirit!
Who was so firm, so constant, that this coil[88]
Would not infect his reason?

ARIEL: Not a soul
But felt a fever of the mad[89] and played
Some tricks of desperation. All but mariners
Plunged in the foaming brine and quit the vessel,
Then all afire with me: the King's son Ferdinand,
With hair up-staring[90]—then like reeds, not hair—
Was the first man that leapt, cried, 'Hell is empty,
And all the devils are here.'

PROSP: Why, that's my spirit!
But was not this nigh[91] shore?

ARIEL: Close by, my master.

PROSP: But are they, Ariel, safe?

ARIEL: Not a hair perished;
On their sustaining garments† not a blemish,
But fresher than before; and as thou bad'st[92] me,
In troops[93] I have dispersed them 'bout the isle.
The King's son have I landed by himself,
Whom I left cooling of[94] the air with sighs
In an odd angle[95] of the isle, and sitting,
His arms in this sad knot.†

[80]*other spirits*

[81]*Presented*

[82]*in precise detail*

[83]*prow; the front end of the ship*

[84]*the middle of the ship*

[85]*produced terror*

[86]*separately*

[87]*faster than the eye can see*

[88]*turmoil*

[89]*a fever like madmen feel*

[90]*standing on end*

[91]*near*

[92]*ordered, commanded*

[93]*groups*

[94]*cooling off*

[95]*section, corner*

PROSP: Of the King's ship,
The mariners, say how thou hast disposed,
And all the rest o'th' fleet.
ARIEL: Safely in harbour
Is the King's ship, in the deep nook where once
Thou calld'st me up at midnight to fetch dew
From the still vexed[96] Bermudas, there she's hid;
The mariners all under hatches stowed
Who, with a charm joined to their suffered labour,
I have left asleep; and for the rest o'th' fleet,
Which I dispersed, they all have met again,
And are upon the Mediterranean float,[97]
Bound sadly home for Naples,
Supposing that they saw the King's ship wrecked,
And his great person perish.
PROSP: Ariel, thy charge
Exactly is performed; but there's more work.
What is the time o'th' day?
ARIEL: Past the mid season.[98]
PROSP: At least two glasses.[99] The time 'twixt six and now
Must by us both be spent most preciously.
ARIEL: Is there more toil? Since thou dost give me pains[100]
Let me remember thee what thou hast promised,
Which is not yet performed me.
PROSP: How now? Moody?
What is't thou canst demand?
ARIEL: My liberty.
PROSP: Before the time be out? No more!
ARIEL: I prithee,
Remember I have done thee worthy service,
Told thee no lies, made thee no mistakings, served
Without or[101] grudge or grumblings. Thou did promise
To bate[102] me a full year.
PROSP: Dost thou forget
From what a torment I did free thee?
ARIEL: No.
PROSP: Thou dost, and think'st it much to tread the ooze
Of the salt deep,
To run upon the sharp wind of the north,
To do me business in the veins o'th' earth
When it is baked with frost.
ARIEL: I do not, sir.

[96]constantly stormy
[97]sea
[98]noon
[99]two hourglasses; two hours
[100]jobs, tasks
[101]either
[102]excuse

Prosp: Thou liest, malignant thing! Hast thou forgot
The foul witch Sycorax, who with age and envy
Was grown into a hoop?[103] Hast thou forgot her?
Ariel: No, sir.
Prosp: Thou hast. Where was she born? Speak; tell me.
Ariel: Sir, in Algiers.
Prosp: O, was she so? I must
Once in a month recount what thou hast been,
Which thou forget'st. This damned witch Sycorax,
For mischiefs manifold and sorceries terrible
To enter human hearing, from Algiers
Thou know'st was banished—for one thing she did
They would not take her life.† Is not this true?
Ariel: Ay, sir.
Prosp: This blue-eyed hag was hither brought with child,
And here was left by th' sailors. Thou, my slave,
As thou report'st thyself, wast then her servant;
And for thou wast a spirit too delicate
To act her earthy and abhorred commands,
Refusing her grand hests,[104] she did confine thee,
By help of her more potent ministers[105]
And in her most unmitigable rage,
Into a cloven pine; within which rift
Imprisoned thou didst painfully remain
A dozen years; within which spaced she died
And left thee there, where thou didst vent thy groans
As fast as mill-wheels strike.[106] Then was this island—
Save for the son that she did litter here,
A freckled whelp, hag-born—not honoured with
A human shape.
Ariel: Yes, Caliban her son.
Prosp: Dull thing, I say so: he, that Caliban
Whom now I keep in service. Thou best know'st
What torment I did find thee in. Thy groans
Did make wolves howl, and penetrate[107] the breasts
Of ever-angry bears; it was a torment
To lay upon the damned, which Sycorax
Could not again undo. It was mine art,
When I arrived and heard thee, that made gape
The pine and let thee out.
Ariel: I thank thee, master.
Prosp: If thou more murmur'st, I will rend an oak,

[103] a hunchback; bent over with age

[104] urgent commands

[105] slaves

[106] hit the water

[107] arouse sympathy in

And peg thee in his knotty entrails till
Thou hast howled away twelve winters.
ARIEL: Pardon, master.
I will be correspondent to command
And do my spiriting gently.[108]
PROSP: Do so, and after two days
I will discharge thee.
ARIEL: That's my noble master!
What shall I do? Say what; what shall I do?
PROSP: Go make thyself like a nymph o'th' sea.
Be subject to no sight by thine and mine, invisible
To every eyeball else. Go take this shape,
And hither come in't: go; hence with diligence!
[Exit Ariel]
Awake, dear heart, awake! Thou hast slept well;
Awake.
MIRAN: The strangeness of your story put
Heaviness[109] in me.
PROSP: Shake it off. Come on;
We'll visit Caliban my slave, who never
Yields us kind answer.
MIRAN: 'Tis a villain, sir,
I do not love to look on.
PROSP: But as 'tis,
We cannot miss[110] him: he does make our fire,
Fetch in our wood, and serves in offices[111]
That profit us. What ho! Slave, Caliban!
Thou earth, thou, speak!
CALIBAN: *[within]* There's wood enough within.
PROSP: Come forth, I say! There's other business for thee.
Come, thou tortoise! When?
[Re-enter Ariel like a water-nymph]
Fine apparition! My quaint Ariel,
Hark in thine ear.
ARIEL: My lord, it shall be done. *[Exit]*
PROSP: Thou poisonous slave, got by the devil himself
Upon thy wicked dam,[112]† come forth!

[Enter Caliban]
CALIBAN: As wicked dew as e'er my mother brushed[113]
With raven's feather from unwholesome fen†[114]
Drop on you both! A south-west blow on ye

[108] *graciously*
[109] *Drowsiness*
[110] *do without*
[111] *duties, tasks*
[112] *mother*
[113] *collected*
[114] *bog, swamp*

And blister you all o'er!†
PROSP: For this be sure tonight thou shalt have cramps,
Side-stiches that shall pen thy breath up. Urchins
Shall, for that vast of night that they may work,
All exercise on thee. Thou shalt be pinched
As thick as honeycomb,† each pinch more stinging
Than bees that made 'em.
CALIBAN: I must eat my dinner.
This island's mine, by Sycorax my mother,
Which thou tak'st from me. When thou cam'st first,
Thou strok'st me and made much of me, wouldst give me
Water and berries in't, and teach me how
To name the bigger light, and how the less,†
That burn by day and night; and then I loved thee,
And showed thee all the qualities o'th' isle,
The fresh springs, brine-pits, barren place and fertile—
Cursed be I that did so! All the charms
Of Sycorax, toads, beetles, bats, light on you!
For I am all the subjects that you have,
Which first was mine own king, and here you sty me[115]
In this hard rock, whiles you do keep from me
The rest o'th' island.
PROSP: Thou most lying slave,
Whom stripes[116] may move, not kindness! I have used
thee,
Filth as thou art, with human care, and lodged thee
In mine own cell, till thou didst seek to violate
The honour of my child.
CALIBAN: O ho, O ho! Would't had been done!
Thou didst prevent me; I had peopled else
This isle with Calibans.
MIRANDA:† Abhorrèd slave,
Which any print[117] of goodness wilt not take,
Being capable of all ill! I pitied thee,
Took pains to make thee speak, taught thee each hour
One thing or other. When thou didst not, savage,
Know thine own meaning, but wouldst gabble like
A thing most brutish, I endowed thy purposes
With words that made them known. But thy vile race,
Though thou didst learn, had that in't which good natures
Could not abide to be with; therefore wast thou
Deservedly confined into this rock,

[115]*pen me up like a pig*

[116]*whips, lashes*

[117]*imprint, impression*

Who hadst deserved more than a prison.
CALIBAN: You taught me language, and my profit on't
Is I know how to curse. The red plague[†] rid you
For learning me your language!
PROSP: Hag-seed,[†] hence!
Fetch us in fuel, and be quick, thou'rt best,
To answer other business.—Shrug'st thou, malice?
If thou neglect'st or dost unwillingly
What I command, I'll rack thee with old cramps,
Fill all thy bones with aches, make thee roar,
That beasts shall tremble at thy din.[118]
CALIBAN: No, pray thee.
[Aside] I must obey. His art is of such power,
It would control my dam's god Setebos,[†]
And make a vassal of him.
PROSP: So, slave, hence! *[Exit Caliban]*

[Re-enter Ariel, invisible, playing and singing; Ferdinand following]

ARIEL: *[sings]*
Come unto these yellow sands,
And then take hands;
Curtsied when you have and kissed—
The wild waves whist[119]—
Foot it featly[120] here and there,
And, sweet sprites, bear[121]
The burden.[122] Hark, hark!
SPIRITS: [dispersedly] Bow-wow!
ARIEL: The watch-dogs bark.
SPIRITS: [dispersedly] Bow-wow!
ARIEL: Hark, hark! I hear
The strain of strutting Chanticleer[123]
Cry 'cock-a-diddle-dow.'

FERD: Where should this music be? I'th' air or th' earth?
It sounds no more; and sure it waits upon
Some god o'th' island. Sitting on a bank,
Weeping again the King my father's wreck,
This music crept by me upon the waters,
Allaying both their fury and my passion
With its sweet air.[124] Thence I have followed it,

[118] *noise*

[119] *be silent*

[120] *dance it elegantly*

[121] *sing*

[122] *verse, refrain*

[123] *rooster*

[124] *tune, melody*

Or it hath drawn me rather. But 'tis gone.
No, it begins again.

ARIEL: *[sings]*

Full fathom five thy father lies.
Of his bones are coral made;
Those are pearls that were his eyes;
Nothing of him that doth fade
But doth suffer a sea-change
Into something rich and strange.
Sea-nymphs hourly ring his knell:

SPIRITS: Ding dong.

ARIEL: Hark, now I hear them,—Ding-dong bell.

FERD: The ditty does remember my drowned father.
This is no mortal business, nor no sound
That the earth owes.[125]—I hear it now above me.

PROSP: *[to Miranda]* The fringèd curtains of thine eye advance
And say what thou seest yond.

MIRAN: What is't? A spirit?
Lord, how it looks about! Believe me, sir,
It carries a brave[126] form. But 'tis a spirit.

PROSP: No, wench, it eats and sleeps, and hath such senses
As we have, such. This gallant which thou seest
Was in the wreck, and but he's something[127] stained
With grief, that's beauty's canker,† thou mightest call him
A goodly person. He hath lost his fellows,
And strays about to find 'em.

MIRAN: I might call him
A thing divine, for nothing natural
I ever saw so noble.

PROSP: *[Aside]* It[128] goes on, I see,
As my soul prompts it. *[to Ariel]* Spirit, fine spirit, I'll free thee
Within two days for this.

FERD: *[Aside]* Most sure, the goddess
On whom these airs attend! *[to Miranda]* Vouchsafe my prayer
May know if you remain upon this island,
And that you will some good instruction give
How I may bear me[129] here. My prime request,
Which I do last pronounce, is—O you wonder!—
If you be maid† or no?

[125] *owns*

[126] *splendid, gallant*

[127] *somewhat*

[128] *My plan*

[129] *conduct myself*

MIRAN: No wonder, sir,
But certainly a maid.
FERD: My language! Heavens!
I am the best of them that speak this speech,
Were I but where 'tis spoken.
PROSP: How? The best?
What wert thou if the King of Naples heard thee?
FERD: A single thing, as I am now, that wonders
To hear thee speak of Naples. He does hear me,
And that he does I weep; myself am Naples,[130]
Who with mine eyes, never since at ebb,[131] beheld
The King my father wrecked.
MIRAN: Alack, for mercy!
FERD: Yes, faith, and all his lords, the Duke of Milan
And his brave son being twain.
PROSP: *[Aside]* The Duke of Milan
And his more braver daughter could control thee,
If now 'twere fit to do't. At the first sight
They have changed eyes.† Delicate Ariel,
I'll set thee free for this *[to Ferdinand]* A word, good sir.
I fear you have done yourself some wrong;† a word.
MIRAN: *[Aside]* Why speaks my father so urgently? This
Is the third man that e'er I saw, the first
That e'er I sighed for. Pity move my father
To be inclined my way!
FERD: O, if a virgin,
And your affection not gone forth,[132] I'll make you
The Queen of Naples.
PROSP: Soft, sir! One word more.
[Aside] They are both in either's powers; but this swift business
I must uneasy[133] make, lest too light[134] winning
Make the prize light. *[to Ferdinand]* One word more; I charge thee
That thou attend me. Thou dost here usurp
The name thou ow'st[135] not; and hast put thyself
Upon this island as a spy, to win it
From me, the lord on't.
FERD: No, as I am a man.
MIRAN: There's nothing ill can dwell in such a temple:
If the ill spirit have so fair a house,
Good things will strive to dwell with't.

[130] *King of Naples*
[131] *constantly weeping*
[132] *is not promised to someone else*
[133] *difficult*
[134] *easy, cheap*
[135] *own*

Prosp: *[to Ferdinand]* Follow me.
[to Miranda] Speak not you for him; he's a traitor.
[to Ferdinand] Come,
I'll manacle thy neck and feet together.
Sea-water shalt thou drink; thy food shall be
The fresh-brook mussels,† withered roots, and husks
Wherein the acorn cradled. Follow.

Ferd: No;
I will resist such entertainment[136] till
Mine enemy has more power.
[He draws, and is charmed from moving]

Miran: O dear father,
Make not too rash a trial of him, for
He's gentle, and not fearful.

Prosp: What, I say,
My foot[137] my tutor? Put thy sword up, traitor,
Who mak'st a show but dar'st not strike, thy conscience
Is so possessed with guilt. Come from thy ward,
For I can here disarm thee with this stick
And make thy weapon drop.

Miran: Beseech you, father!—

Prosp: Hence! Hang not on my garments.

Miran: Sir, have pity;
I'll be his surety.

Prosp: Silence! One word more
Shall make me chide thee, if not hate thee. What,
An advocate for an imposter? Hush!
Thou think'st there is no more such shapes as he,
Having seen but him and Caliban. Foolish wench!
To th' most of men this is a Caliban,
And they to him are angels.

Miran: My affections
Are then most humble. I have no ambition
To see a goodlier man.

Prosp: *[to Ferdinand]* Come on; obey.
Thy nerves[138] are in their infancy again,
And have no vigour in them.

Ferd: So they are.
My spirits,[139] as in a dream, are all bound up.
My father's loss, the weakness which I feel,
The wreck of all my friends, nor this man's threats,
To whom I am subdued, are but light to me,

[136]*treatment*

[137]*inferior*

[138]*muscles, tendons*

[139]*mind*

Might I but through my prison once a day
Behold this maid. All corners else o'th' earth
Let liberty make use of; space enough
Have I in such a prison.

PROSP: *[Aside]* It works. *[to Ariel]* Come on.—
Thou has done well, fine Ariel. *[to Ferdinand]* Follow
me.
[to Ariel] Hark what thou else shalt do me.

MIRAN: *[to Ferdinand]* Be of comfort.
My father's of a better nature, sir,
Than he appears by speech. This is unwonted[140]
Which now came from him.

PROSP: *[to Ariel]* Thou shalt be free
As mountain winds; but then[141] exactly do
All points of my command.

ARIEL: To th' syllable.

PROSP: *[to Ferdinand]*
Come, follow. *[to Miranda]* Speak not for him.

[Exeunt]

[140] *unusual, strange*

[141] *until then*

ACT II

SCENE I

Another part of the island.

[Enter Alonso, Sebastian, Antonio, Gonzalo, Adrian, and Francisco]

GONZ: *[to Alonso]* Beseech you, sir, be merry. You have cause,
So have we all, of joy; for our escape
Is much beyond our loss. Our hint of woe
Is common; every day some sailor's wife,
The masters of some merchant, and the merchant†
Have just our theme of woe; but for the miracle,
I mean our preservation, few in millions
Can speak like us. Then wisely, good sir, weigh
Our sorrow with our comfort.
ALONSO: Prithee, peace.†
SEBAST: He receives comfort like cold porridge.
ANTONIO: The visitor† will not give him o'er[1] so.
SEBAST: Look, he's winding up the watch of his wit. By and by it will strike.
GONZ: *[to Alonso]* Sir,—
SEBAST: *[to Antonio]* One: tell.[2]
GONZ: *[to Alonso]* —when every grief is entertained that's offered,
Comes to th' entertainer—
SEBAST: A dollar.
GONZ: Dolour[3] comes to him indeed. You have spoken truer than you
purposed.
SEBAST: You have taken it wiselier than I meant you should.
GONZ: *[to Alonso]* Therefore, my lord,—
ANTONIO: *[to Sebastian]* Fie, what a spendthrift is he of his tongue!
ANLONSO: *[to Gonzalo]* I prithee, spare.[4]

[1]*leave him alone*

[2]*keep count*

[3]*Sorrow*

[4]*spare your words*

GONZ: Well, I have done. But yet—

SEBAST: *[to Antonio]* He will be talking.

ANTONIO: Which, of he or Adrian, for a good wager, first begins to crow?[5]

SEBAST: The old cock.

ANTONIO: The cockerel.

SEBAST: Done. The wager?

ANTONIO: A laughter.

SEBAST: A match!

ADRIAN: *[to Gonzalo]* Though this island seem to be desert,[6]—

ANTONIO: *[to Sebastian]* Ha, ha, ha!

SEBAST: So, you're paid.†

ADRIAN: Uninhabitable, and almost inaccessible—

SEBAST: *[to Antonio]* Yet—

ADRIAN: Yet–

ANTONIO: *[to Sebastian]* He could not miss't.

ADRIAN: It must needs be of subtle,[7] tender, and delicate temperance.[8]

ANTONIO: *[to Sebastian]* Temperance† was a delicate wench.

SEBAST: Ay, and a subtle, as he most learnedly delivered.

ADRIAN: *[to Gonzalo]* The air breathes upon us here most sweetly.

SEBAST: *[to Antonio]* As if it had lungs, and rotten ones.

ANTONIO: Or as 'twere perfumed by a fen.[9]

GONZ: *[to Adrian]* Here is everything advantageous to life.

ANTONIO: *[to Sebastian]* True, save[10] means to live.

SEBAST: Of that there's none, or little.

GONZ: *[to Adrian]* How lush and lusty[11] the grass looks! How green!

ANTONIO: The ground indeed is tawny.

SEBAST: With an eye[12] of green in't.

ANTONIO: He misses not much.

SEBAST: No, he doth but mistake the truth totally.

GONZ: *[to Adrian]* But the rarity of it is, which is indeed almost beyond credit—

SEBAST: *[to Antonio]* As many vouched[13] rarities are.

GONZ: *[to Adrian]* That our garments, being, as they were, drenched in the sea, hold notwithstanding their freshness and glosses, being rather new-dyed than stained with salt water.

[5]*speak*

[6]*uninhabited*

[7]*gentle*

[8]*climate, weather*

[9]*bog, marsh*

[10]*except*

[11]*luxuriant*

[12]*hint, tinge, shade*

[13]*accepted*

ANTONIO: *[to Sebastian]* If but one of his pockets could speak, would it not say he lies?

SEBAST: Ay, or very falsely pocket up his report.

GONZ: *[to Adrian]* Methinks our garments are now as fresh as when we put them on first in Afric, at the marriage of the King's fair daughter Claribel to the King of Tunis.

SEBAST: 'Twas a sweet marriage, and we prosper well in our return.

ADRIAN: Tunis was never graced before with such a paragon to[14] their queen.

GONZ: Not since widow Dido's† time.

ANTONIO: Widow? A pox o'that! How came that widow in? Widow Dido!

SEBAST: What if he had said 'widower Aeneas' too? Good Lord, how you take it!

ADRIAN: *[to Gonzalo]* 'Widow Dido' said you? You make me study of[15] that: she was of Carthage, not of Tunis.

GONZ: This Tunis, sir, was Carthage.

ADRIAN: Carthage?

GONZ: I assure you, Carthage.

ANTONIO: *[to Sebastian]* His word is more than the miraculous harp.†

SEBAST: He hath raised the wall, and houses too.

ANTONIO: What impossible matter will he make easy next?

SEBAST: I think he will carry this island home in his pocket and give it his son for an apple.

ANTONIO: And sowing the kernels[16] of it in the sea, bring forth more islands.

GONZ: *[to Adrian]* Ay.†

ANTONIO: *[to Sebastian]* Why, in good time.

GONZ: *[to Alonso]* Sir, we were talking that our garments seem now as fresh as when we were at Tunis at the marriage of your daughter, who is not queen.

ANTONIO: And the rarest that e'er came there.

SEBAST: Bate,[17] I beseech you, widow Dido.

ANTONIO: O, widow Dido! Ay, widow Dido.

GONZ: *[to Alonso]* Is not, sir, my doublet as fresh as the first day I wore it? I mean, in a sort.

ANTONIO: *[to Sebastian]* That sort was well fished for.

GONZ: *[to Alonso]* When I wore it at your daughter's marriage.

ALONSO: You cram these words into mine ears against

[14] *for*

[15] *examine*

[16] *seeds*

[17] *Except*

The stomach of my sense.† Would I have never
Married my daughter there! For, coming thence,
My son is lost, and, in my rate,[18] she too,
Who is so far from Italy removed
I ne'er again shall see her. O thou mine heir
Of Naples and of Milan, what strange fish
Hath made his meal on thee?

Francis: Sir, he may live.
I saw him beat the surges under him
And ride upon their backs; he trod the water,
Whose enmity he flung aside, and breasted
The surge most swoll'n that met him; his bold head
'Bove the contentious waves he kept, and oared
Himself with his good arms in lusty[19] stroke
To th' shore, that o'er his wave-worn basis bowed,†
As[20] stooping to relieve him: I not doubt
He came alive to land.

Alonso: No, no; he's gone.

Sebast: *[to Alonso]* Sir, you may thank yourself for this great loss,
That would not bless our Europe with your daughter,
But rather lose her to an African,
Where she, at least, is banished from your eye,
Who hath cause to wet the grief on't.

Alonso: Prithee, peace.

Sebast: You were kneeled to an importuned otherwise
By all of us, and the fair soul herself
Weighed between loathness and obedience at
Which end o'th' beam should bow.† We have lost your son,
I fear, for ever. Milan and Naples have
More widows in them of this business' making
Than we bring men to comfort them.
That fault's your own.

Alonso: So is the dear'st o'th' loss.

Gonz: My lord Sebastian,
The truth you speak doth lack some gentleness
And time to speak it in—you rub the sore,
When you should bring the plaster.†

Sebast: Very well.

Antonio: And most chirurgeonly.[21]

[18] *opinion, estimation*

[19] *strong, vigorous*

[20] *As if*

[21] *like a surgeon*

GONZ: *[to Alonso]* It is foul weather in us all, good sir,
When you are cloudy.
SEBAST: *[to Antonio]* Foul weather?
ANTONIO: Very foul.
GONZ: *[to Alonso]* Had I plantation of this isle, my lord,—
ANTONIO: *[to Sebastian]* He'd sow't with nettle-seed.
SEBAST: Or docks, or mallows.
GONZ: And were the king on't, what would I do?
SEBAST: *[to Antonio]* 'Scape being drunk, for want of wine.
GONZ: I'th' commonwealth I would by contraries
Execute all things, for no kind of traffic[22]
Would I admit; no name of magistrate;
Letters should not be known; riches, poverty,
And use of service,[23] none; contract, succession,
Bourn,[24] bound of land, tilth,[25] vineyard, none;
No use of metal, corn, or wine, or oil;
No occupation; all men idle, all;
And women too, but innocent and pure;
No sovereignty—
SEBAST: *[to Antonio]* Yet he would be king on't.
ANTONIO: The latter end of his commonwealth forgets the beginning.
GONZ: *[to Alonso]* All things in common[26] nature should produce
Without sweat or endeavour. Treason, felony,
Sword, pike, knife, gun, or need of any engine,[27]
Would I not have; but nature should bring forth,
Of it own kind, all foison,[28] all abundance,
To feed my innocent people.
SEBAST: *[to Antonio]* No marrying 'mong his subjects?
ANTONIO: None, man; all idle: whores and knaves.
GONZ: *[to Alonso]* I would with such perfection govern, sir,
T'excel the golden age.†
SEBAST: Save[29] his majesty!
ANTONIO: Long live Gonzalo!
GONZ: *[to Alonso]* And—do you mark me, sir?
ALONSO: Prithee, no more. Thou dost talk nothing to me.
GONZ: I do well believe your highness, and did it to minister occasion[30] to these gentlemen, who are of such sensible[31] and nimble lungs that they always use to laugh at nothing.
ANTONIO: 'Twas you we laughed at.

[22] *business*
[23] *servants*
[24] *Limit*
[25] *cultivation*
[26] *communal*
[27] *weapon*
[28] *plenty (a plentiful harvest)*
[29] *God save*
[30] *to give an opportunity (to laugh)*
[31] *sensitive*

GONZ: Who, in this kind of merry fooling, am nothing to you; so you may continue and laugh at nothing still.

ANTONIO: What a blow was there given!

SEBAST: An it had not fallen flat-long.[32]†

[32]*harmlessly*

GONZ: You are gentlemen of brave mettle;† you would lift the moon out of her sphere, if she would continue in it five weeks without changing.

[Enter Ariel, invisible, playing solemn music]

SEBAST: We would so, and then go a-bat-fowling.†

ANTONIO: *[to Gonzalo]* Nay, good my lord, be not angry.

GONZ: No, I warrant you; I will not adventure my discretion so weakly.† Will you laugh me asleep, for I am very heavy?[33]

[33]*tired*

ANTONIO: Go sleep, and hear us.

[All sleep except Alonso, Sebastian, and Antonio]

ALONSO: What, all so soon asleep? I wish mine eyes
Would, with themselves, shut up my thoughts: I find
They are inclined to do so.

SEBAST: Please you, sir,
Do not omit[34] the heavy offer of it.
It seldom visits sorrow; when it doth,
It is a comforter.

[34]*disregard*

ANTONIO: We two, my lord,
Will guard your person while you take your rest,
And watch your safety.

ALONSO: Thank you. Wondrous heavy.

[Alonso sleeps. Exit Ariel]

SEBAST: What a strange drowsiness possesses them!

ANTONIO: It is the quality o'th' climate.

SEBAST: Why
Doth it not then our eyelids sink? I find not
Myself disposed to sleep.

ANTONIO: Nor I; my spirits are nimble.
They fell together all, as by consent;
They dropped, as by a thunder-stroke. What might,
Worthy Sebastian, O, what might–? No more!—
And yet methinks I see it in thy face,
What thou shouldst be. Th' occasion speaks[35] thee, and
My strong imagination sees a crown

[35]*the opportunity reveals to*

Dropping upon thy head.
SEBAST: What, art thou waking?[36]
ANTONIO: Do you not hear me speak?
SEBAST: I do; and surely
It is a sleepy language and thou speak'st
Out of thy sleep. What is it thou didst say?
This is a strange repose, to be asleep
With eyes wide open; standing, speaking, moving,
And yet so fast asleep.
ANTONIO: Noble Sebastian,
Thou let'st thy fortune sleep—die rather; wink'st[37]
Whiles thou art waking.
SEBAST: Thou dost snore distinctly;
There's meaning in thy snores.
ANTONIO: I am more serious than my custom. You
Must be so too, if heed me; which to do
Trebles thee o'er.†
SEBAST: Well, I am standing water.[38]
ANTONIO: I'll teach you how to flow.
SEBAST: Do so: to ebb
Hereditary sloth† instructs me.
ANTONIO: O,
If you but knew how you the purpose cherish
Whiles thus you mock it;† how in stripping it[39]
You more invest[40] it! Ebbing[41] men, indeed,
Most often do so near the bottom run
By their own fear or sloth.
SEBAST: Prithee, say on.
The setting[42] of thine eye and cheek proclaim
A matter[43] from thee, and a birth, indeed,
Which throes[44] thee much to yield.[45]
ANTONIO: Thus, sir:
Although this lord[46] of weak remembrance, this,
Who shall be of as little memory
When he is earth'd,[47] hath here almost persuaded—
For he's a spirit of persuasion, only
Professes to persuade[48]—the king his son's alive,
'Tis as impossible that he's undrowned
As he that sleeps here swims.
SEBAST: I have no hope
That he's undrowned.
ANTONIO: O, out of that 'no hope'

[36]*awake*

[37]*close your eyes*

[38]*waiting to be moved*

[39]*putting it off*

[40]*the more important it becomes*

[41]*Declining*

[42]*expression*

[43]*Importance*

[44]*pains*

[45]*to bear*

[46]*Gonzalo*

[47]*buried*

[48]*his only occupation is to provide advice*

What great hope have you! No hope that way is
Another way so high a hope that even
Ambition cannot pierce a wink[49] beyond,
But doubt discovery there.† Will you grant with me
That Ferdinand is drowned?

Sebast: He's gone.

Antonio: Then, tell me,
Who's the next heir of Naples?

Sebast: Claribel.

Antonio: She that is Queen of Tunis; she that dwells
Ten leagues beyond man's life;[50] she that from Naples
Can have no note,[51] unless the sun were post[52]—
The man i'th' moon's too slow—till new-born chins
Be rough and razorable; she that from[53] whom
We all were sea-swallowed, though some cast[54] again,
And by that destiny, to perform an act
Whereof what's past is prologue; what to come
In yours and my discharge.[55]†

Sebast: What stuff is this? How say you?
'Tis true my brother's daughter's Queen of Tunis;
So is she heir of Naples; 'twixt which regions
There is some space.

Antonio: A space whose every cubit
Seems to cry out, 'How shall that Claribel
Measure us back to Naples? Keep in Tunis,
And let Sebastian wake.'[56] Say this were death
That now hath seized them; why, they were no worse
Than now they are. There be that[57] can rule Naples
As well as he that sleeps, lords that can prate
As amply and unnecessarily
As this Gonzalo; I myself could make
A chough of as deep chat.† O, that you bore
The mind that I do! what a sleep were this
For your advancement! Do you understand me?

Sebast: Methinks I do.

Antonio: And how does your content
Tender[58] your own good fortune?

Sebast: I remember
You did supplant your brother Prospero.

Antonio: True;
And look how well my garments sit upon me,
Much feater[59] than before. My brother's servants

[49] *catch a glimpse*
[50] *farther than any man travels in his lifetime*
[51] *information*
[52] *a messenger*
[53] *returning from*
[54] *cast ashore*
[55] *performance*
[56] *wake up to his opportunity*
[57] *those that*
[58] *take care of; regard*
[59] *neater*

Were then my fellows; now they are my men.
SEBAST: But for your conscience?
ANTONIO: Ay, sir, where lies that? If 'twere a kibe,
'Twould put me to my slipper, but I feel not
This deity in my bosom.† Twenty consciences
That stand 'twixt me and Milan, candied[60] be they
And melt ere they molest![61] Here lies your brother,
No better than the earth he lies upon
If he were that which now he's like—that's dead;
Whom I with this obedient steel,[62] three inches of it,
Can lay to bed for ever; whiles you, doing thus,†
To the perpetual wink of aye[63] might put
This ancient morsel, this Sir Prudence, who
Should not upbraid our course. For all the rest,
They'll take suggestion[64] as a cat laps milk;
They'll tell the clock[65] to any business that
We say befits the hour.
SEBAST: Thy case, dear friend,
Shall be my precedent: as thou got'st Milan,
I'll come by Naples. Draw thy sword—one stroke
Shall free thee from the tribute which thou payest,
And I the King shall love thee.
ANTONIO: Draw together,
And when I rear my hand, do you the like,
To fall it on Gonzalo.
SEBAST: O, but one word. *[They talk apart]*

[Enter Ariel, invisible, with music and song]

ARIEL: *[to Gonzalo]* My master through his art foresees the danger
That you, his friend, are in, and sends me forth—
For else[66] his project dies—to keep them[67] living.
[Ariel sings in Gonzalo's ear]

While you here do snoring lie,
Open-eyed conspiracy
His time[68] doth take.
If of life you keep a care,
Shake off slumber, and beware.
Awake, awake!

ANTONIO: *[to Sebastian]* Then let us both be sudden.

[60] *hardened*
[61] *interfere*
[62] *sword*
[63] *neverending sleep*
[64] *temptation to do evil*
[65] *agree*
[66] *otherwise*
[67] *Gonzalo and Alonso*
[68] *chance, opportunity*

GONZ: Now, good angels
Preserve the King.
ALONSO: *[waking]* Why, how now? Ho, awake!
[to Antonio and Sebastian] Why are you[69] drawn?
[to Gonzalo] Wherefore this ghastly[70] looking?
GONZ: What's the matter?
SEBAST: Whiles we stood here securing[71] your repose,
Even now, we heard a hollow burst of bellowing,
Like bulls, or rather lions. Did't not wake you?
It struck mine ear most terribly.
ALONSO: I heard nothing.
ANTONIO: O, 'twas a din to fright a monster's ear,
To make an earthquake! Sure, it was the roar
Of a whole herd of lions.
ALONSO: Heard you this, Gonzalo?
GONZ: Upon mine honour, sir, I heard a humming,
And that a strange one too, which did awake me.
I shaked you, sir, and cried. As mine eyes opened
I saw their weapons drawn. There was a noise,
That's verily.[72] 'Tis best we stand upon our guard,
Or that we quit this place. Let's draw our weapons.
ALONSO: Lead off this ground, and let's make further search
For my poor son.
GONZ: Heavens keep him from these beasts!
For he is sure i'th' island.
ALONSO: Lead away. *[Exeunt all but Ariel]*
ARIEL: Prospero my lord shall know what I have done.
So, King, go safely on to seek thy son.

[Exit]

[69] *your swords*
[70] *frightened*
[71] *guarding*
[72] *the truth*

SCENE II
Another part of the island

[Enter Caliban carrying a burden of wood]

CALIBAN: All the infections that the sun sucks up
From bogs, fens, flats,[1] on Prosper fall, and make him
By inch-meal[2] a disease! *[A noise of thunder heard]*[†]
His spirits hear me,

[1] *swamps, marshes*
[2] *inch by inch*

And yet I needs must curse. But they'll nor pinch,
Fright me with urchin-shows,[3] pitch me i'th' mire,
Nor lead me, like a firebrand in the dark
Out of my way, unless he bid 'em; but
For every trifle are they set upon me,
Sometime like apes that mow[4] and chatter at me
And after bite me, then like hedgehogs, which
Lie tumbling in my barefoot way and mount
Their pricks at my footfall; sometime am I
All wound with adders[5] who with cloven tongues
Do hiss me into madness.

[Enter Trinculo]

Lo, now, lo!
Here comes a spirit of his, and to torment me
For bringing wood in slowly, I'll fall flat.
Perchance he will not mind me.

TRINC: Here's neither bush nor shrub to bear off any weather at all, and another storm brewing. I hear it sing i'th' wind. Yon same black cloud, yon huge one, looks like a foul bombard that would shed his liquor. If it should thunder as it did before, I know now where to hide my head. Yon same cloud cannot choose but fall by pailfuls. *[sees Caliban]* What have we here—a man or a fish?—dead or alive? A fish: he smells like a fish; a very ancient and fish-like smell; a kind of not-of-the-newest Poor-John.[6] A strange fish! Were I in England now, as once I was, and had but this fish painted,† not a holiday-fool there but would give a piece of silver. There would this monster make a man.† Any strange beast there makes a man. When they will not give a dolt[7] to relieve a lame beggar, they will lay out ten to see a dead Indian.† Legged like a man, and his fins like arms! Warm o'my troth! I do now let loose my opinion; hold it no longer: this is no fish, but an islander that hath lately suffered[8] by a thunderbolt. *[Thunder]* Alas, the storm is come again! My best way is to creep under his gaberdine;[9] there is no other shelter heareabout. Misery acquaints a man with strange bedfellows. I will here shroud[10] till the dregs of the storm be past.

[He crawls under Caliban's cloak]

[Enter Stephano, singing, a bottle in his hand]

STEPH: I shall no more to sea, to sea,

[3] *spirits appearing like hedgehogs*

[4] *scowl*

[5] *venomous snakes*

[6] *a dried, salty fish*

[7] *a coin*

[8] *perished*

[9] *cloak*

[10] *take cover, hide*

Here shall I die ashore—
This is a very scurvy tune to sing at a man's funeral. Well, here's my comfort. *[Drinks]*

[Sings]

The master, the swabber, the boatswain, and I,
The gunner and his mate,
Loved Mall, Meg, and Marian, and Margery,
But none of us cared for Kate;
For she had a tongue with a tang,[11]
Would cry to a sailor, 'Go hang!'
She loved not the savour of tar nor of pitch,
Yet a tailor might scratch her where'er she did itch:
Then to sea, boys, and let her go hang!
This is a scurvy tune too: but here's my comfort.
[Drinks]

CALIBAN: *[to Trinculo]* Do not torment me! O!

STEPH: What's the matter? Have we devils here? Do you put tricks upon's with savages and men of Ind,[12] ha? I have not scaped drowning to be afeard now of your four legs; for it hath been said, 'As proper a man as ever went on four legs cannot make him give ground.' And it shall be said so again, while Stephano breathes at nostrils.

CALIBAN: The spirits torments me. O!

STEPH: This is some monster of the isle with four legs, who hath got, as I tak it, an ague.[13] Where the devil should he learn our language? I will give him some relief, if it be but for that. If I can recover him and keep him tame and get to Naples with him, he's a present for any emperor that ever trod on neat's leather.[14]

CALIBAN: *[to Trinculo]* Do not torment me, prithee! I'll bring my wood home faster.

STEPH: He's in his fit now, and does not talk after the wisest.[15] He shall taste of my bottle. If he have never drunk wine afore, it will go near to remove his fit. If I can recover him and keep him tame, I will not take too much for him. He shall pay for him that hath[16] him, and that soundly.

CALIBAN: *[to Trinculo]* Thou dost me yet but little hurt. Thou wilt anon, I know it by thy trembling. Now Prosper works upon thee.

[11] *sting*
[12] *India*
[13] *a fever*
[14] *shoes*
[15] *in a wise way*
[16] *gets*

STEPH: Come on your ways. Open your mouth. Here is that which will give language to you, cat. Open your mouth. This will shake[17] your shaking, I can tell you, and that soundly. You cannot tell who's your friend. Open your chaps again.

[Caliban drinks]

TRINC: I should know that voice. It should be—but he is drowned, and these are devils. O, defend me!

STEPH: Four legs and two voices—a most delicate[18] monster! His forward voice now is to speak well of his friend; his backward voice is to utter foul speeches and to detract. If all the wine in my bottle will recover him, I will help his ague. Come. *[Caliban drinks]* Amen![19] I will pour some in thy other mouth.

TRINC: Stephano!

STEPH: Doth thy other mouth call me? Mercy, mercy! This is a devil, and no monster. I will leave him. I have no long spoon.†

TRINC: Stephano! If thou beest Stephano, touch me and speak to me, for I am Trinculo—be not afeard—thy good friend Trinculo.

STEPH: If thou beest Trinculo, come forth. I'll pull thee by the lesser legs. If any be Trinculo's legs, these are they. *[He pulls Trinculo out from under Caliban's cloak by the legs]* Thou art very Trinculo indeed! How cam'st thou to be the siege[20] of this moon-calf?† can he vent[21] Trinculos?

TRINC: I took him to be killed with a thunder-stroke. But art thou not drowned, Stephano? I hope now thou art not drowned. Is the storm overblown? I hid me under the dead moon-calf's gaberdine for fear of the storm. And art thou living, Stephano? O Stephano, two Neapolitans† scaped!

STEPH: Prithee, do not turn me about;† my stomach is not constant.

CALIBAN: *[Aside]* These be fine things, an if they be not sprites.
That's a brave god and bears celestial liquor.
I will kneel to him.†

STEPH: *[to Trinculo]* How didst thou 'scape? How cam'st thou hither? Swear by this bottle how thou cam'st hither. I escaped upon a butt of sack[22] which the sailors heaved o'erboard—by this bottle, which I made of the bark of a tree with mine own hands since I was cast ashore.

CALIBAN: I'll swear upon that bottle to be thy true subject, for the liquor is not earthly.

[17] *stop*

[18] *exquisitely made*

[19] *Enough*

[20] *excrement*

[21] *defecate*

[22] *a cask of wine*

STEPH: *[offering the bottle to Trinculo]* Here. Swear then how thou escapedst.

TRINC: Swum ashore, man, like a duck. I can swim like a duck, I'll be sworn.

STEPH: Here, kiss the book.† Though thou canst swim like a duck, thou art made like a goose.†

TRINC: O Stephano, hast any more of this?

STEPH: The whole butt,[23] man. My cellar is in a rock by th' seaside where my wine is hid. *[Caliban rises]* How now, moon-calf, how does thine ague?

[23]*cask, container*

CALIBAN: Hast thou not dropped from heaven?

STEPH: Out o'th' moon, I do assure thee: I was the man i'th' moon when time was.[24]

[24]*once upon a time*

CALIBAN: I have seen thee in her, and I do adore thee. My mistress showed me thee and thy dog and thy bush.†

STEPH: Come, swear to that. Kiss the book. I will furnish it anon with new contents. Swear.

TRINC: By this good light, this is a very shallow monster! I afeard of him? A very weak monster! The man i'th' moon? A most poor, credulous monster! Well drawn,[25] monster, in good sooth!

[25]*drunk*

CALIBAN: I'll show thee every fertile inch o'th' island;
And I will kiss thy foot. I prithee, be my god.

TRINC: By this light, a most perfidious and drunken monster! When's god's asleep, he'll rob his bottle.

CALIBAN: I'll kiss thy foot. I'll swear myself thy subject.

STEPH: Come on then; down, and swear.

TRINC: I shall laugh myself to death at this puppy-headed monster. A most scurvy monster! I could find in my heart to beat him—

STEPH: Come, kiss.

TRINC: But that the poor monster's in drink. An abominable monster!

CALIBAN: I'll show thee the best springs; I'll pluck thee berries;
I'll fish for thee, and get thee wood enough.
A plague upon the tyrant that I serve!
I'll bear him no more sticks, but follow thee,
Thou wondrous man.

TRINC: A most ridiculous monster, to make a wonder of a poor drunkard!

CALIBAN: I prithee, let me bring thee where crabs[26] grow;

[26]*crab apples*

And I with my long nails will dig thee pignuts,[27]
Show thee a jay's nest, and instruct thee how
To snare the nimble marmoset, I'll bring thee
To clustering filberts, and sometimes I'll get thee
Young sea-mews[28] from the rock. Wilt thou go with me?

STEPH: I prithee now, lead the way without any more talking.—Trinculo, the King and all our company else being drowned, we will inherit here. Here, bear my bottle. Fellow Trinculo, we'll fill him by and by again.

CALIBAN: *[sings drunkenly]* Farewell, master, farewell, farewell!

TRINC: A howling monster, a drunken monster!

CALIBAN: *[sings]*

No more dams I'll make for fish
Nor fetch in firing[29]
At requiring,
Nor scrape trenchering, nor wash dish
'Ban, 'Ban, Cacaliban
Has a new master—get a new man!†

Freedom high-day! High-day, freedom! Freedom, high-day, freedom!

STEPH: O brave monster! Lead the way.

[Exeunt]

[27]*chestnuts*

[28]*seagulls*

[29]*wooden plates*

ACT III

SCENE I
Before Prospero's Cell.

[Enter Ferdinand, bearing a log]

FERD: There be some sports are painful, and their labour
Delight in them sets off.† Some kinds of baseness,
Are nobly undergone, and most poor matters
Point to rich ends. This my mean[1] task
Would be as heavy to me as odious, but
The mistress which I serve quickens what's dead
And makes my labours pleasures. O, she is
Ten times more gentle than her father's crabbed,
And he's composed of harshness. I must remove
Some thousands of these logs and pile them up,
Upon a sore[2] injunction. My sweet mistress
Weeps when she sees me work, and says such baseness
Had never like executor.† I forget,[3]
But these sweet thoughts do even refresh my labours,
Most busil'est, when I do it.

[1]lowly

[2]harsh

[3]forget to work

[Enter Miranda. Prospero enters at a distance, unseen]

MIRANDA: Alas now, pray you,
Work not so hard. I would the lightning had
Burnt up those logs that you are enjoined to pile!
Pray, set it down, and rest you. When this burns,
'Twill weep for having wearied you.† My father
Is hard at study. Pray now, rest yourself.
He's safe for these three hours.

FERD: O most dear mistress,
The sun will set before I shall discharge
What I must strive to do.

MIRANDA: If you'll sit down

I'll bear your logs the while. Pray, give me that;
I'll carry it to the pile.

FERD: No, precious creature.
I had rather crack my sinews, break my back,
Than you should such dishonour undergo,
While I sit lazy by.

MIRANDA: It would become me
As well as it does you; and I should do it
With much more ease, for my good will is to it,
And yours it is against.

PROSP: *[aside]* Poor worm, thou art infected!
This visitation shows it.†

MIRANDA: You look wearily.

FERD: No, noble mistress, 'tis fresh morning with me
When you are by at night. I do beseech you—
Chiefly that I might set it in my prayers—
What is your name?

MIRANDA: Miranda. O my father,
I have broke your hest[4] to say so!

FERD: Admired Miranda!†
Indeed the top of admiration, worth
What's dearest to the world! Full many a lady
I have eyed with best regard, and many a time
Th' harmony of their tongues hath into bondage
Brought my too diligent ear. For several virtues
Have I liked several women; never any
With so full soul, but some defect in her
Did quarrel with the noblest grace she owed[5]
And put it to the foil.[6] But you, O you,
So perfect and so peerless, are created
Of every creature's best!

MIRANDA: I do not know
One of my sex; no woman's face remember
Save from my glass,[7] mine own; nor have I seen
More that I may call men than you, good friend,
And my dear father. How features are abroad,
I am skilless[8] of; but, by my modesty,[9]
The jewel in my dower, I would not wish
Any companion in the world but you;
Nor can imagination form a shape
Besides[10] yourself to like of. But I prattle
Something too wildly, and my father's precepts

[4] *disobeyed your request*

[5] *owned*

[6] *challenge (as in fencing)*

[7] *mirror*

[8] *ignorant*

[9] *virginity, purity*

[10] *Equal to*

I therein do forget.
Ferd: I am in my condition
A prince, Miranda; I do think, a king—
I would[11] not so!—and would no more endure
This wooden slavery† than to suffer
The flesh-fly† blow my mouth. Hear my soul speak:
The very instant that I saw you did
My heart fly to your service; there resides
To make me slave to it; and for your sake
Am I this patient log-man.
Miranda: Do you love me?
Ferd: O heaven, O earth, bear witness to this sound,
And crown what I profess with kind event
If I speak true! If hollowly[12] invert
What best is boded[13] me to mischief![14] I,
Beyond all limit of what else i'th' world,
Do love, prize, honour you.
Miranda: *[weeping]* I am a fool
To weep at what I am glad of.
Prosp: *[aside]* Fair encounter
Of two most rare affections! Heavens rain grace
On that which breeds between 'em!
Ferd: Wherefore weep you?
Miran: At mine unworthiness that dare not offer
What I desire to give, and much less take
What I shall die to want. But this is trifling,
And all the more it seeks to hide itself
The bigger bulk it shows. Hence, bashful cunning!
And prompt me, plain and holy innocence!
I am your wife, if you will marry me.
If not, I'll die your maid: to be your fellow[15]
You may deny me, but I'll be your servant
Whether you will or no.
Ferd: My mistress, dearest;
And I thus humble ever.
Miran: My husband then?
Ferd: Ay, with a heart as willing
As bondage e'er of freedom: here's my hand.†
Miran: And mine, with my heart in't, and now farewell
Till half an hour hence.
Ferd: A thousand thousand!
[Exeunt Ferdinand and Miranda severally[16]]

[11] *wish it were*
[12] *insincerely*
[13] *foretold to*
[14] *evil, misfortune*
[15] *equal*
[16] *separately*

PROSP: So glad of this as they I cannot be,
Who are surprised withal, but my rejoicing
At nothing can be more. I'll to my book,
For yet ere supper-time must I perform
Much business appertaining. *[Exit]*

SCENE II

Another part of the island.

[Enter Caliban, Stephano, and Trinculo drunk]

STEPH: *[to Caliban]* Tell not me.† When the butt is out we will drink water—not a drop before. Therefore, bear up, and board 'em: Servant-monster, drink to me.

TRINC: Servant-monster? The folly of this island! They say there's but five upon this isle: we are three of them; if th'other two be brained like us, the state totters.[1]

[1] *shakes, staggers*

STEPH: Drink, servant-monster, when I bid thee. Thy eyes are almost set[2] in thy head.

[2] *fixed drunkenly*

TRINC: Where should they be set else? He were a brave monster indeed, if they were set in his tail

STEPH: My man-monster hath drowned his tongue in sack. For my part, the sea cannot drown me. I swam, ere I could recover the shore, five and thirty leagues off and on. By this light, thou shalt be my lieutenant, monster, or my standard.[3]

[3] *standard-bearer†*

TRINC: Your lieutenant, if you list,[4] he's no standard.

[4] *wish*

STEPH: We'll not run, Monsieur Monster.

TRINC: Nor go neither; but you'll lie like dogs and yet say nothing neither.

STEPH: Moon-calf, speak once in thy life, if thou beest a good moon-calf.

CALIBAN: How does thy honour? Let me lick thy shoe. I'll not serve him; he's not valiant.

TRINC: Thou liest, most ignorant monster! I am in case[5] to jostle a constable. Why, thou debauched fish, thou, was there ever man a coward that hath drunk so much sack as I to-day? Wilt thou tell a monstrous lie, being but half a fish and half a monster?

[5] *prepared*

CALIBAN: *[to Stephano]* Lo, how he mocks me! Wilt thou let him, my lord?

TRINC: 'Lord' quoth he! That a monster should be such a natural![6]†

CALIBAN: *[to Stephano]* Lo, lo, again! Bite him to death, I prithee.

STEPH: Trinculo, keep a good tongue in your head. If you prove a mutineer, the next tree!† The poor monster's my subject, and he shall not suffer indignity.

CALIBAN: I thank my noble lord. Wilt thou be pleased to hearken once again to the suit I made to thee?

STEPH: Marry, will I. Kneel and repeat it. I will stand, and so shall Trinculo. *[Caliban kneels]*

[Enter Ariel, invisible]

CALIBAN: As I told thee before, I am subject to a tyrant, a sorcerer, that by his cunning hath cheated me of the island.

ARIEL: Thou liest.

CALIBAN: Thou liest, thou jesting monkey, thou.
I would my valiant master would destroy thee!
I do not lie.

STEPH: Trinculo, if you trouble him any more in's tale, by this hand, I will supplant[7] some of your teeth.

TRINC: Why, I said nothing.

STEPH: Mum, then, and no more. *[to Caliban]* Proceed.

CALIBAN: I say, by sorcery he got this isle;
From me he got it. If thy greatness will
Revenge it on him—for I know thou dar'st,
But this thing† dare not—

STEPH: That's most certain.

CALIBAN: Thou shalt be lord of it, and I'll server thee.

STEPH: How now shall this be compassed?[8] Canst thou bring me to the party?[9]

CALIBAN: Yea, yea, my lord. I'll yield him thee asleep
Where thou mayst knock a nail into his head.†

ARIEL: Thou liest; thou canst not.

CALIBAN: What a pied ninny's this! *[to Trinculo]* Thou scurvy patch![10]
[to Stephano] I do beseech thy greatness give him blows,
And take this bottle from him. When that's gone

[6] *idiot*

[7] *uproot*

[8] *completed, accomplished*

[9] *Prospero*

[10] *fool, idiot*

He shall drink nought brine, for I'll not show him
Where the quick freshes[11] are.

Steph: Trinculo, run into no further danger: interrupt the monster one word further, and, by this hand, I'll turn my mercy out o'doors and make a stockfish of thee.

Trinc: Why, what did I? I did nothing. I'll go farther off.

Steph: Didst thou not say he lied?

Ariel: Thou liest.

Steph: Do I so? Take thou that. *[Beating Trinculo]* As you like this, give me the lie[12] another time.

Trinc: I did not give the lie. Out o'your wits and hearing too? A pox o'your bottle! This can sack and drinking do. A murrain[13] on your monster, and the devil take your fingers!

Caliban: Ha, ha, ha!

Steph: Now, forward with your tale. *[to Trinculo]* Prithee, stand farther off.

Caliban: Beat him enough; after a little time
I'll beat him too.

Steph: *[to Trinculo]* Stand farther. *[to Caliban]* Come, proceed.

Caliban: Why, as I told thee, 'tis a custom with him,
I'th' afternoon to sleep. There thou mayst brain him,
Having first seized his books, or with a log,
Batter his skull, or paunch[14] him with a stake,
Or cut his wezand[15] with thy knife. Remember
First to possess his books, for without them
He's but a sot,[16] as I am, nor hath not
One spirit to command—they all do hate him
As rootedly as I. Burn but his books.
He has brave utensils,[17] for so he calls them,
Which when he has a house, he'll deck withal.
And that most deeply to consider is
The beauty of his daughter. He himself
Calls her a nonpareil.[18] I never saw a woman,
But only Sycorax my dam and she;
But she as far surpasseth Sycorax
As great'st does least.

Steph: Is it so brave[19] as lass?

Caliban: Ay, lord; she will become thy bed, I warrant.
And bring thee forth brave brood.

Steph: Monster, I will kill this man. His daughter and I will

[11] *fast flowing freshwater springs*

[12] *call me a liar*

[13] *plague*

[14] *to stab, usually in the stomach*

[15] *windpipe*

[16] *an ignorant fool*

[17] *tools*

[18] *one with no equal*

[19] *excellent*

be king and queen—save[20] our graces!—and Trinculo and thyself shall be viceroys.
Dost thou like the plot, Trinculo?

TRINC: Excellent.

STEPH: *[to Trinculo]* Give me thy hand. I am sorry I beat thee; but, while thou liv'st, keep a good tongue in thy head.

CALIBAN: Within this half hour will he be asleep.
Wilt thou destroy him then?

STEPH: Ay, on mine honour.

ARIEL: *[aside]* This will I tell my master.

CALIBAN: Thou mak'st me merry; I am full of pleasure.
Let us be jocund. Will you troll[21] the catch[22]
You taught me but while-ere?[23]

STEPH: At thy request, monster, I will do reason, any reason.[24]
Come on,
Trinculo, let us sing.
[Sings]

Flout 'em and scout 'em, And scout 'em and flout 'em
Thought is free.

CALIBAN: That's not the tune.

[Ariel plays the tune on a tabour and pipe]

STEPH: What is this same?

TRINC: This is the tune of our catch, played by the picture of Nobody.†

STEPH: *[calling toward Ariel]* If thou beest a man, show thyself in thy likeness. If thou beest a devil, take't as thou list.[25]

TRINC: O, forgive me my sins!

STEPH: He that dies pays all debts. *[Calling out]* I defy thee.—Mercy upon us!

CALIBAN: Art thou afeared?

STEPH: No, monster, not I.

CALIBAN: Be not afeard. The isle is full of noises,
Sounds and sweet airs, that give delight and hurt not.
Sometimes a thousand twangling instruments
Will hum about mine ears, and sometime voices
That, if I then had waked after long sleep,
Will make me sleep again: and then, in dreaming,
The clouds methought would open and show riches
Ready to drop upon me, that when I waked
I cried to dream again.

[20] *God save*

[21] *sing*

[22] *song*

[23] *a short while ago*

[24] *anything within reason*

[25] *wish*

STEPH: This will prove a brave kingdom to me, where I shall have my music for nothing.

CALIBAN: When Prospero is destroyed.

STEPH: That shall be by and by.[26] I remember the story.

[26] very soon

[Exit Ariel, playing music]

TRINC: The sound is going away. Let's follow it, and after do our work.

STEPH: Lead, monster; we'll follow. I would I could see this tabourer. He lays it on.

TRINC: Wilt come? I'll follow, Stephano. *[Exeunt]*

SCENE III

Another part of the island.

[Enter Alonso, Sebastian, Antonio, Gonzalo, Adrian, and Francisco]

GONZALO: *[to Alonso]* By'r lakin,† I can go no further, sir.
My old bones ache. Here's a maze trod indeed
Through forthrights and meanders![1] By your patience,
I needs must rest me.

[1] both direct and winding paths

ALONSO: Old lord, I cannot blame thee,
Who am myself attached[2] with weariness,
To th' dulling of my spirits. Sit down and rest.
Even here I will put off my hope, and keep it
No longer for my flatterer. He is drowned
Whom thus we stray to find, and the sea mocks
Our frustrate search on land. Well, let him go.

[2] seized

[They sit]

ANTONIO: *[aside to Sebastian]* I am right glad that he's so out of hope.
Do not for one repulse forgo the purpose
That you resolved t'effect.

SEBASTIAN: *[aside to Antonio]* The next advantage
Will we take throughly.[3]

[3] thoroughly

ANTONIO: *[aside to Sebastian]* Let it be tonight;
For now they are oppressed with travel. They
Will not, nor cannot, use such vigilance
As when they are fresh

SEBASTIAN: *[aside to Antonio]* I say tonight. No more.

[Solemn and strange music]

[Enter Prospero, invisible]

ALONSO: What harmony is this? My good friends, hark!
GONZALO: Marvellous sweet music!

[Enter several strange shapes, bringing in a banquet; they dance about it with gentle actions of salutation; and, inviting the King and his companions to eat, they depart]

ALONSO: Give us kind keepers,[4] heavens! What were these?
SEBASTIAN: A living drollery. Now I will believe
That there are unicorns, that in Arabia
There is one tree, the phoenix' throne, one phoenix
At this hour reigning there.
ANTONIO: I'll believe both;
And what does else want credit,[5] come to me,
And I'll be sworn 'tis true. Travellers ne'er did lie,
Though fools at home condemn 'em.
GONZALO: If in Naples
I should report this now, would they believe me—
If I should say I saw such islanders?
For certes[6] these are people of the island,
Who, though they are of monstrous shape, yet note,
Their manners are more gentle-kind than of
Our human generation you shall find
Many, nay, almost any.
PROSP: *[aside]* Honest lord,
Thou hast said well, for some of you there present
Are worse than devils.
ALONSO: I cannot too much muse.[7]
Such shapes, such gesture, and such sound, expressing—
Although they want the use of tongue,[8] a kind
Of excellent dumb discourse.
PROSP: *[aside]* Praise in departing.†
FRANCISCO: They vanished strangely.
SEBASTIAN: No matter, since
They have left their viands[9] behind, for we have stomachs.
Will't please you taste of what is here?
ALONSO: Not I.
GONZALO: Faith, sir, you need not fear. When we were boys,
Who would believe that there were mountaineers
Dewlapped like bulls, whose throats had hanging at 'em

[4]*guardian angels*

[5]*anything else unbelievable*

[6]*certainly*

[7]*marvel*

[8]*language*

[9]*food*

Wallets of flesh? Or that there were such men
Whose heads stood in their breasts? Which now we find
Each putter-out of five for one† will bring us
Good warrant of.

Alonso: I will stand to and feed,
Although my last—no matter, since I feel
The best is past. Brother, my lord the Duke,
Stand to, and do as we.

[Alonso, Sebastian, and Antonio approach the table.]

[Thunder and lightning. Enter Ariel, like a harpy,† claps his wings upon the table, and, with a quaint device, the banquet vanishes]

Ariel: You are three men of sin, whom Destiny,
That hath to[10] instrument this lower world
And what is in't, the never-surfeited sea
Hath caused to belch up you, and on this island
Where man doth not inhabit, you 'mongst men
Being most unfit to live. I have made you mad,
And even with suchlike valour[11] men hang and drown
Their proper selves.

[Alonso, Sebastian, and Antonio draw their swords]

You fools! I and my fellows
Are ministers of Fate. The elements,
Of whom your swords are tempered, may as well
Wound the loud winds, or with bemocked-at stabs
Kill the still-closing waters, as diminish
One dowl that's in my plume. My fellow ministers
Are like invulnerable. If you could hurt,
Your swords are now too massy for your strengths
And will not be uplifted.

[Alonso, Sebastian, and Antonio stand bewildered]

But remember,
For that's my business to you, that you three
From Milan did supplant good Prospero;
Exposed unto the sea, which hath requit it,
Him and his innocent child; for which foul deed,
The powers, delaying, not forgetting, have
Incensed the seas and shores, yea, all the creatures,
Against your peace. Thee of thy son, Alonso,
They have bereft, and do pronounce by me

[10] *as/its*

[11] *fearlessness from insanity*

Lingering perdition,† worse than any death
Can be at once, shall step by step attend
You and your ways; whose wraths to guard you from—
Which here in this most desolate isle else falls
Upon your heads—is nothing but heart's sorrow
And a clear life ensuing.
[He vanishes in thunder; then, to soft music, enter the shapes again, and dance with mocks and mows,[12] and carrying out the table]

PROSP: Bravely the figure of this harpy hast thou
Performed, my Ariel; a grace it had devouring.
Of my instruction hast thou nothing bated[13]
In what thou hast to say. So, with good life
And observation strange, my meaner ministers[14]
Their several kinds have done.[15] My high charms work,
And these mine enemies are all knit up
In their distractions. They now are in my power,
And in these fits I leave them, while I visit
Young Ferdinand, whom they suppose is drowned,
And his and mine loved darling. *[Exit above]*

GONZALO: I'th' name of something holy sir, why stand you
In this strange stare?

ALONSO: O, it is monstrous, monstrous!
Methought the billows spoke and told me of it,
The winds did sing it to me, and the thunder,
That deep and dreadful organ-pipe, pronounced
The name of Prosper. It did bass my trespass.
Therefore my son i'th' ooze is bedded, and
I'll seek him deeper than e'er plummet sounded,
And with him there lie mudded. *[Exit]*

SEBASTIAN: But one fiend at a time,
I'll fight their legions o'er.[16]

ANTONIO: I'll be thy second.
[Exeunt Sebastian and Antonio]

GONZALO: All three of them are desperate. Their great guilt,
Like poison given to work a great time after,
Now 'gins to bite the spirits. I do beseech you
That are of suppler joints, follow them swiftly,
And hinder them from this ecstasy[17]
May now provoke them to.

ADRIAN: Follow, I pray you.
[Exeunt]

[12] *grimaces*

[13] *omitted*

[14] *lesser spirits*

[15] *performed*

[16] *from beginning to end*

[17] *madness*

ACT IV

SCENE I

Before Prospero's cell.

[Enter Prospero, Ferdinand, and Miranda]

Prosp: *[to Ferdinand]* If I have too austerely punished you,
Your compensation makes amends, for I
Have given you here a third of mine own life—
Or that for which I live—who once again
I tender[1] to thy hand. All thy vexations
Were but my trials of thy love, and thou
Hast strangely[2] stood the test. Here, afore Heaven,
I ratify this my rich gift. O Ferdinand,
Do not smile at me that I boast of her,
For thou shalt find she will outstrip all praise,
And make it halt behind her.

Ferd: I do believe it
Against an oracle.†

Prosp: Then, as my gift and thine own acquisition
Worthily purchased[3] take my daughter. But
If thou dost break her virgin-knot before
All sanctimonious ceremonies may
With full and holy rite be ministered,
No sweet aspersion[4] shall the heavens let fall
To make this contract grow; but barren hate,
Sour-eyed disdain and discord shall bestrew
The union of your bed with weeds† so loathly
That you shall hate it both; therefore, take heed,
As Hymen's† lamps shall light you.

Ferd: As I hope
For quiet days, fair issue[5] and long life
With such love as 'tis now, the murkiest den,
The most opportune place, the strong'st suggestion[6]
Our worser genius can, shall never melt

[1]*offer*
[2]*wonderfully*
[3]*gained*
[4]*shower, sprinkle*
[5]*children*
[6]*temptation*

Mine honour into lust to take away
The edge[7] of that day's celebration
When I shall think: or Phoebus' steeds are foundered,
Or Night kept chained below.[†]

PROSP: Fairly spoke.
Sit then, and talk with her. She is thine own.
What, Ariel! My industrious servant, Ariel!

[Enter Ariel]

ARIEL: What would my potent master? Here I am.

PROSP: Thou and thy meaner fellows your last service
Did worthily perform, and I must use you
In such another trick. Go bring the rabble,[8]
O'er whom I give thee power, here to this place.
Incite them to quick motions; for I must
Bestow upon the eyes of this young couple
Some vanity[9] of mine art. It is my promise,
And they expect it from me.

ARIEL: Presently?

PROSP: Ay, with a twink.[10]

ARIEL: Before you can say 'Come' and 'Go,'
And breathe twice and cry 'So, so,'
Each one, tripping on his toe
Will be here with mop and mow.
Do you love me, master? No?

PROSP: Dearly, my delicate Ariel. Do not approach
Till thou dost hear me call.

ARIEL: Well, I conceive. *[Exit]*

PROSP: *[to Ferdinand]* Look thou be true. Do not give dalliance
Too much the rein: the strongest oaths are straw
To th' fire i'th' blood. Be more abstemious,
Or else, good night your vow!

FERD: I warrant you, sir;
The white cold virgin snow upon my heart
Abates the ardour of my liver.

PROSP: Well.—
Now come, my Ariel! Bring a corollary,[11]
Rather than want a spirit. Appear and pertly![12]
[to Ferdinand and Miranda]
No tongue, all eyes! Be silent. *[Soft music]*

[7] *desire*
[8] *lesser fellows*
[9] *display*
[10] *wink of an eye*
[11] *excess, surplus*
[12] *briskly*

[Enter Iris†]

IRIS: Ceres,† most bounteous lady, thy rich leas[13]
Of wheat, rye, barley, vetches, oats and peas;
Thy turfy mountains, where live nibbling sheep,
And flat meads[14] thatched with stover,[15] them to keep;
Thy banks with pioned and twilled[16] brims,
Which spongy April at thy hest betrims,
To make cold nymphs chaste crowns; and thy
broom-groves,
Whose shadow the dismissèd bachelor loves,
Being lass-lorn; thy pole clipped vineyard;
And thy sea-marge,[17] sterile and rocky-hard,
Where thou thyself dost air[18]—the Queen o'th'Sky,†
Whose watery arch[19] and messenger am I,
Bids thee leave these, and with her sovereign grace,
[Juno appears] Here on this grass-plot, in this very place
To come and sport. Her peacocks fly amain.[20]
Approach, rich Ceres, her to entertain.

[Enter Ariel as Ceres]

CERES: Hail, many-coloured messenger, that ne'er
Dost disobey the wife of Jupiter;[21]
Who with thy saffron wings upon my flowers
Diffusest honey-drops, refreshing showers,
And with each end of thy blue bow dost crown
My bosky acres and my unshrubbed down,
Rich scarf to my proud earth. Why hath thy queen
Summoned me hither to this short-grassed green?
IRIS: A contract of true love to celebrate;
And some donation freely to estate[22]
On the blest lovers.
CERES: Tell me, heavenly bow,[23]
If Venus or her son,[24] as thou dost know,
Do now attend the queen. Since they did plot
The means that dusky Dis† my daughter got,
Her and her blind boy's scandaled company
I have forsworn.
IRIS: Of her society
Be not afraid. I met her deity.
Cutting the clouds towards Pathos† and her son

[13]*fertile lands*
[14]*meadows*
[15]*hay*
[16]*entwined*
[17]*seashore*
[18]*get fresh air*
[19]*rainbow*
[20]*quickly; in haste*
[21]*Juno*
[22]*bestow*
[23]*rainbow*
[24]*Cupid*

Dove-drawn† with her. Here thought they to have done
Some wanton charm[25] upon this man and miad,
Whose vows are that no bed-right shall be paid
Till Hymen's torch be lighted—but in vain.
Mars's hot minion[26] is returned again.
Her waspish-headed son has broke his arrows,
Swears he will shoot no more, but play with sparrows†
And be a boy right out.[27] *[Music is heard]*

CERES: High'st queen of state,
Great Juno, comes; I know her by her gait.[28]

[Enter Juno]

JUNO: How does my bounteous sister? Go with me
To bless this twain, that they may Prospus be
And honoured in their issue. *[They sing]*

JUNO:
Honour, riches, marriage-blessing,
Long continuance, and increasing,
Hourly joys be still[29] upon you!
Juno sings her blessings upon you.

CERES:
Earth's increase, foison[30] plenty,
Barns and garners never empty,
Vines and clust'ring bunches growing,
Plants and goodly burden bowing;
Spring come to you at the farthest
In the very end of harvest!†
Scarcity and want shall shun you,
Ceres' blessing so is on you.

FERD: This is a most majestic vision, and
Harmoniously charmingly. May I be bold
To think these spirits?

PROSP: Spirits, which by mine art
I have from their confines call'd to enact
My present fancies.

FERD: Let me live here ever!
So rare a wondered father and a wife
Makes this place paradise.

[Juno and Ceres whisper, and send Iris on employment]

PROSP: Sweet,[31] now, silence!
Juno and Ceres whisper seriously;

[25] *cast a lustful spell*
[26] *lover; Venus*
[27] *an ordinary boy*
[28] *majestic demeanor; way of walking*
[29] *always*
[30] *abundance*
[31] *softly*

There's something else to do. Hush, and be mute,
Or else our spell is marred.

IRIS: Your nymphs, called naiads† of the wandering brooks,
With your sedged crowns[32] and over-harmless looks,
Leave your crisp channels and on this green land
Answer your summons; Juno does command.
Come, temperate nymphs, and help to celebrate
A contract of true love. Be not too late.
[Enter certain nymphs]
You sunburnt sicklemen,[33] of August weary,
Come hither from the furrow and be merry;
Make holiday, your rye-straw hats put on,
And these fresh nymphs encounter every one
In country footing.

[Enter certain reapers, properly habited. They join with the nymphs in a graceful dance; towards the end whereof Prospero starts suddenly, and speaks.

PROSP: *[aside]* I had forgot that foul conspiracy
Of the beast Caliban and his confederates
Against my life. The minute of their plot
Is almost come. *[to the spirits]* Well done! Avoid;[34]
no more!
[To a strange, hollow, and confused noise, the spirits heavily vanish[35]]

FERD: *[to Miranda]* This is strange. Your father's in some
passion
That works[36] him strongly.

MIRANDA: Never till this day
Saw I him touched with anger so distempered.[37]

PROSP: You do look, my son, in a moved sort,[38]
As if you were dismayed. Be cheerful, sir.
Our revels now are ended. These our actors,
As I foretold you, were all spirits, and
Are melted into air, into thin air;
And, like the baseless fabric[39] of this vision,
The cloud-capped towers, the gorgeous palaces,
The solemn temples, the great globe† itself,
Yea, all which it inherit,[40] shall dissolve,
And, like this insubstantial pageant faded,
Leave not a rack[41] behind. We are such stuff

[32] *wreaths (crowns) made of reeds*

[33] *harvesters*

[34] *Begone*

[35] *sorrowfully depart*

[36] *aggravates*

[37] *troubled, distracted*

[38] *disturbed, in a troubled way*

[39] *emptiness; without substance*

[40] *all who come to own (possess) it*

[41] *a trail of cloud*

As dreams are made on, and our little life
Is rounded[42] with a sleep. Sir, I am vexed.
Bear with my weakness. My brain is troubled.
Be not disturbed with my infirmity.
If you be pleased, retire into my cell
And there repose. A turn or two I'll walk
To still my beating mind.

FERD AND MIRANDA: We wish your peace. *[Exeunt]*

PROSP: Come with a thought![43] I thank thee, Ariel. Come!

[Enter Ariel]

ARIEL: Thy thoughts I cleave to. What's thy pleasure?

PROSP: Spirit,
We must prepare to meet with Caliban.

ARIEL: Ay, my commander. When I presented[44] Ceres,
I thought to have told thee of it, but I feared
Lest I might anger thee.

PROSP: Say again: where didst thou leave these varieties?[45]

ARIEL: I told you, sir, they were red-hot with drinking;
So fun of valour that they smote the air
For breathing in their faces, beat the ground
For kissing of their feet; yet always bending[46]
Towards their project. Then I beat my tabour,
At which, like unbacked[47] colts, they pricked their ears,
Advanced[48] their eyelids, lifted up their noses
As they[49] smelt music. So I charmed their ears
That calf-like they my lowing[50] followed through
Toothed briars, sharp furzes, pricking goss[51] and thorns,
Which entered their frail shins. At last I left them
I'th' filthy-mantled[52] pool beyond your cell,
There dancing up to th' chins, that the foul lake
O'er-stunk their feet.

PROSP: This was well done, my bird.[53]
Thy shape invisible retain thou still.
The trumpery[54] in my house, go bring it hither
For stale[55] catch these thieves.

ARIEL: I go, I go. *[Exit]*

PROSP: A devil, a born devil, on whose nature
Nurture can never stick; on whom my pains,
Humanely taken, all, all lost, quite lost,
And, as with age his body uglier grows,

[42] *surrounded, crowned*

[43] *Come as fast as a thought!*

[44] *acted as*

[45] *criminals, ruffians*

[46] *aiming*

[47] *never-ridden*

[48] *Opened*

[49] *As if*

[50] *mooing*

[51] *prickly shrubs*

[52] *filthy, scum-covered*

[53] *dear*

[54] *cheap goods*

[55] *bait*

So his mind cankers.[56] I will plague them all,
Even to roaring.

[Re-enter Ariel, loaden with glistering apparel,[57] etc.]

Come, hang them on this line.

[Ariel hangs up the apparel. Exeunt Prospero and Ariel]

[Enter Caliban, Stephano, and Trinculo, all wet]

CALIBAN: Pray you, tread softly, that the blind mole may not
Hear a foot fall. We now are near his cell.

STEPH: Monster, you fairy, which you say is a harmless fairy, has done little better than played the Jack[58] with us.

TRINC: Monster, I do smell[59] all horse-piss, at which my nose is in great indignation.

STEPH: So is mine. Do you hear, monster? If I should take a displeasure against you, look you—

TRINC: Thou wert but a lost monster.

CALIBAN: Good my lord, give me thy favour still.
Be patient, for the prize[60] I'll bring thee to
Shall hoodwink[61] this mischance. Therefore speak softly.
All's hushed as midnight yet.

TRINC: Ay, but to lose our bottles in the pool!

STEPH: There is not only disgrace and dishonour in that, monster, but an infinite loss.

TRINC: That's more to me than my wetting. Yet this is your harmless fairy, monster.

STEPH: I will fetch off[62] my bottle, though I be o'er ears[63] for my labour.

CALIBAN: Prithee, my king, be quiet. Seest thou here;
This is the mouth o'th' cell. No noise, and enter.
Do that good mischief which may make this island
Thine own for ever, and I, thy Caliban,
For aye[64] thy foot-licker.

STEPH: Give me thy hand. I do begin to have bloody thoughts.

TRINC: *[seeing the apparel]* O King Stephano! O peer! O worthy Stephano!
Look what a wardrobe here is for thee!

CALIBAN: Let it alone, thou fool; it is but trash.

TRINC: *[putting on a garment]* O, ho, monster! We know what belongs to flippers.[65] O King Stephano!

STEPH: Put off that gown, Trinculo. By this hand, I'll have that gown.

[56]*festers*

[57]*the bait*

[58]*villain*

[59]*smell of*

[60]*loot, merchandise*

[61]*blind (with a hood)*

[62]*recover, find*

[63] *drowned*

[64]*ever*

[65] *a second-hand shop*

Trinc: Thy grace shall have it.
Caliban: The dropsy† drown this fool! What do you mean
To dote thus on such luggage?[66] Let't alone,
And do the murder first. If he awake,
From toe to crown he'll fill our skins with pinches,
Make us strange stuff.
Steph: Be you quiet, monster. Mistress lime,[67] is not this my jerkin?[68] Now is the jerkin under the line.† Now, jerkin, you are like to lose your hair and prove a bald jerkin.
Trinc: Do, do! We steal by line and level,† an't like[69] your grace.
Steph: I thank thee for that jest. Here's a garment for't. Wit shall not go unrewarded while I am king of this country. 'Steal by line and level' is an excellent pass of pate.[70]† There's another garment for't.
Trinc: Monster, come, put some lime upon your fingers,† and away with the rest.
Caliban: I will have none on't. We shall lose our time,
And all be turned to barnacles, or to apes
With foreheads villanous[71] low.
Steph: Monster, lay to[72] your fingers. Help to bear this away where my hogshead of wine is, or I'll turn you out of my kingdom. Go to, carry this.
Trinc: And this.
Steph: Ay, and this. *[They load Caliban with the apparel]*

[A noise of hunters heard. Enter divers[73] spirits in the shape of dogs and hounds, and hunting them about; Prospero and Ariel setting them on]

Prosp: Hey, Mountain, hey!
Ariel: Silver! I there it goes, Silver!
Prosp: Fury, Fury! There, Tyrant, there! Hark! Hark!
[Exeunt Stephano, Trinculo, and Caliban followed by spirits]
[to Ariel] Go, charge my goblins that they grind their joints
With dry convulsions, shorten up their sinews,
With aged cramps, and more pinch-spotted† make them
Than pard or cat o'mountain.†
Ariel: Hark, they roar!

[66] burdens
[67] lime tree
[68] leather jacket
[69] if it please
[70] "Thrust of wit"
[71] wretchedly
[72] apply to
[73] various

PROSP: Let them be hunted soundly.[74] At this hour
Lie at my mercy all mine enemies.
Shortly shall all my labours end, and thou
Shalt have the air at freedom. For a little
Follow, and do me service.

[Exeunt]

[74]*thoroughly*

ACT V

SCENE I

Before Prospero's cell.

[Enter Prospero in his magic robes, and Ariel]

Prosp: Now does my project gather to a head.
My charms crack not, my spirits obey, and time
Goes upright with his carriage.[†] How's the day?
Ariel: On the sixth hour; at which time, my lord,
You said our work should cease.
Prosp: I did say so
When first I raised the tempest. Say, my spirit,
How fares the King and's followers?
Ariel: Confined together
In the same fashion as you gave in charge,
Just as you left them; all prisoners, sir
In the lime-grove which weather-fends[1] your cell;
They cannot budge till your release. The King,
His brother and yours, abide all three distracted,[2]
And the remainder mourning over them,
Brimful of sorrow and dismay; but chiefly
Him that you termed, sir, 'the good old lord Gonzalo:
His tears run down his beard like winter's drops
From eaves of reeds.[3] Your charm so strongly works 'em
That if you now beheld them your affections
Would become tender.
Prosp: Dost thou think so, spirit?
Ariel: Mine would, sir, were I human.
Prosp: And mine shall
Hast thou, which art but air, a touch, a feeling
Of their afflictions, and shall not myself,
One of their kind, that relish all as sharply
Passion as they,[†] be kindlier moved than thou art?
Though with their high[4] wrongs I am struck to th' quick,

[1] *is sheltered from the weather*

[2] *out of their minds; crazy*

[3] *thatched roofs*

[4] *great*

Yet with my nobler reason 'gainst my fury
Do I take part.[5] The rarer action is
In virtue than in vengeance. They being penitent,
The sole drift of my purpose doth extend
Not a frown further. Go release them, Ariel.
My charms I'll break, their senses I'll restore,
And they shall be themselves.

ARIEL: I'll fetch them, sir. *[Exit]*

[Prospero draws a magic circle with his staff]

PROSP: Ye elves of hills, brooks, standing lakes and groves,
And ye that on the sands with printless foot
Do chase the ebbing Neptune and do fly him
When he comes back; you demi-puppets that
By moonshine do the green sour ringlets[6]† make,
Whereof the ewe not bites, and you whose pastime
Is to make midnight mushrooms, that rejoice
To hear the solemn curfew;† by whose aid,
Weak masters† though ye be, I have bedimmed
The noontide sun, called forth the mutinous winds,
And 'twixt the green sea and the azured vault[7]
Set roaring war—to the dread rattling thunder
Have I given fire, and rifted[8] Jove's stout oak
With his own bolt; the strong-based promontory
Have I made shake, and by the spurs[9] plucked up
The pine and cedar: graves at my command
Have waked their sleepers, oped, and let 'em forth
By my so potent art. But this rough magic
I here abjure. And, when I have required[10]
Some heavenly music—which even now I do—
To work mine end upon their senses that
This airy charm is for, I'll break my staff,
Bury it certain fathoms in the earth,
And deeper than did ever plummet sound
I'll drown my book.† *[Solemn music]*

[Re-enter Ariel, followed by Alonso, with a frantic gesture, attended by Gonzalo; Sebastian and Antonio in like manner, attended by Adrian and Francisco. They all enter the circle which Prospero had made, and there stand charmed; which Prospero observing, speaks]

[to Alonso] A solemn air,[11] and the best comforter
To an unsettled fancy,[12] cure thy brains,
Now useless, boiled within thy skull.

[5] *side*

[6] *fairy rings*

[7] *sky of blue*

[8] *split*

[9] *roots*

[10] *summoned*

[11] *song*

[12] *imagination*

[to Sebastian and Antonio] There stand,
For you are spell-stopped.—
Holy Gonzalo, honourable man,
Mine eyes, even sociable[13] to the show[14] of thine,
Fall fellowly drops. *[aside]* The charm dissolves apace,
And as the morning steals upon the night,
Melting the darkness, so their rising senses
Begin to chase the ignorant fumes[15] that mantle[16]
Their clearer reason.—O good Gonzalo,
My true preserver, and a loyal sir
To him you follow'st! I will pay[17] thy graces
Home[18] both in word and deed. Most cruelly
Didst thou, Alonso, use me and my daughter.
Thy brother was a furtherer[19] in the act—
Thou art pinched[20] for't now, Sebastian.
[to Antonio] Flesh and blood,
You, brother mine, that entertained ambition,
Expelled remorse and nature; whom, with Sebastian—
Whose inward pinches therefore are most strong,—
Would here have killed your king; I do forgive thee,
Unnatural though thou art. *[Aside]* Their understanding
Begins to swell, and the approaching tide
Will shortly fill the reasonable shore
That now lie foul and muddy. Not one of them
That yet looks on me, or would know me—Ariel,
Fetch me the hat and rapier in my cell:
I will discase[21] me, and myself present
As I was sometime Milan.[22] Quickly, spirit!
Thou shalt ere long be free.

[Ariel sings and helps to attire him as Duke of Milan]

ARIEL: Where the bee sucks, there suck I:
In a cowslip's bell I lie;
There I couch when owls do cry.
On the bat's back I do fly
After summer merrily.
Merrily, merrily shall I live now
Under the blossom that hangs on the bough.

PROSP: Why, that's my dainty Ariel! I shall miss thee,
But yet thou shalt have freedom—So, so, so.—
To the King's ship, invisible as thou art!

[13] *sympathetic*

[14] *appearance*

[15] *fogs of ignorance*

[16] *cover*

[17] *repay*

[18] *Fully*

[19] *accomplice*

[20] *punished, tortured*

[21] *undress*

[22] *Duke of Milan*

There shalt thou find the mariners asleep
Under the hatches. The Master and the Boatswain
Being awake, enforce them to this place,
And presently, I prithee.

Ariel: I drink the air before me, and return
Or ere your pulse twice beat. *[Exit]*

Gonzalo: All torment, trouble, wonder, and amazement
Inhabits here. Some heavenly power guide us
Out of this fearful country!

Prosp: Behold, sir King,
The wrongèd Duke of Milan, Prospero:
For more assurance that a living prince
Does now speak to thee, I embrace thy body;
And to thee and thy company I bid
A hearty welcome. *[He embraces Alonso]*

[23]*Whether*

Alonso: Whe'er[23] thou beest he or no,
Or some enchanted trifle to abuse me,
As late I have been, I not know. Thy pulse
Beats as of flesh and blood; and, since I saw thee,
Th' affliction of my mind amends, with which
I fear a madness held me. This must crave,[24]
An if this be at all[25]—a most strange story.
Thy dukedom I resign, and do entreat
Thou pardon me my wrongs. But how should Prospero
Be living and be here?

[24]*require explanation*

[25]*if this is actually happening*

Prosp: *[to Gonzalo]* First, noble friend,
Let me embrace thine age,[26] whose honour cannot
Be measured or confined. *[He embraces Gonzalo]*

[26]*old body*

Gonzalo: Whither this be
Or be not, I'll not swear.

Prosp: You do yet taste
Some subtilties† o'th' isle that will not let you
Believe things certain.—Welcome, my friends all!
[aside to Sebastian and Antonio]
But you, my brace[27] of lords, were I so minded,
I here could pluck his highness' frown upon you
And justify you traitors. At this time
I will tell no tales.

[27]*pair*

Sebastian: *[aside]* The devil speaks in him.

Prosp: No.
[to Antonio] For you, most wicked sir, whom to call
brother

Would even infect my mouth, I do forgive
Thy rankest fault, all of them, and require
My dukedom of thee, which perforce[28] I know
Thou must restore.

ALONSO: If thou beest Prospero,
Give us particulars of thy preservation;
How thou hast met us here, who three hours since
Were wrecked upon this shore; where I have lost—
How sharp the point of this remembrance is!—
My dear son Ferdinand.

PROSP: I am woe[29] for't, sir.

ALONSO: Irreparable is the loss, and patience
Says it is past her cure.

PROSP: I rather think
You have not sought her help, of whose soft grace[30]
For the like loss I have her sovereign aid,
And rest myself content.

ALONSO: You the like loss?

PROSP: As great to me as late; and supportable
To make the dear loss have I means much weaker
Than you may call to comfort you, for I
Have lost my daughter.

ALONSO: A daughter?
O heavens, that they were living both in Naples,
The king and queen there! That they were, I wish
Myself were mudded in that oozy bed
Where my son lies. When did you lose your daughter?

PROSP: In this last tempest. I perceive these lords
At this encounter do so much admire[31]
That they devour their reason and scarce think
Their eyes do offices of truth, these words
Are natural breath. But howsoe'er you have
Been jostled from your senses, know for certain
That I am Prospero, and that very Duke
Which was thrust forth of Milan, who most strangely
Upon this shore, where you were wrecked, was landed
To be the lord on't. No more yet of this,
For 'tis a chronicle of day by day,
Not a relation for a breakfast, nor
Befitting this first meeting. Welcome, sir.
This cell's my court. Here have I few attendants
And subjects none abroad. Pray you, look in.

[28]*necessarily*

[29]*grieve*

[30]*mercy*

[31]*wonder*

My dukedom since you have given me again,
I will requite you with as good a thing;
At least bring forth a wonder to content ye
As much as me my dukedom.
[Here Prospero discovers Ferdinand and Miranda playing at chess[†]]

[32] *trick me*

Miranda: Sweet lord, you play me false.[32]
Ferd: No, my dear'st love,
I would not for the world.
Miranda: Yes, for a score of kingdoms you should wrangle,
And I would call it fair play.[†]
Alonso: If this prove
A vision of the island, one dear son
Shall I twice lose.
Sebastian: A most high miracle.
Ferd: Though the seas threaten, they are merciful.
I have cursed them without cause. *[He kneels]*
Alonso: Now all the blessings
Of a glad father compass thee about![33]
Arise and say how thou cam'st here.
[Ferdinand rises]

[33] *surround you*

Miranda: O wonder!
How many goodly creatures are there here!
How beauteous mankind is! O brave new world
That has such people in't!
Prosp: 'Tis new to thee.
Alonso: *[to Ferdinand]* What is this maid with whom thou wast at play?
Your eld'st acquaintance cannot be three hours.
Is she the goddess that hath severed us,
And brought us thus together?
Ferd: Sir, she is mortal;
But by immortal providence she's mine.
I chose her when I could not ask my father
For his advice, nor thought I had one. She
Is daughter to this famous Duke of Milan,
Of whom so often I have heard renown,
But never saw before; of whom I have
Received a second life; and second father
This lady makes him to me.
Alonso: I am hers.[†]
But O, how oddly will it sound that I

Must ask my child[34] forgiveness!
PROSP: There, sir, stop.
Let us not burden our remembrance with
A heaviness[35] that's gone.
GONZALO: I have inly wept,
Or should have spoke ere this. Look down, you gods,
And on this couple drop a blessèd crown!
For it is you that have chalked forth[36] the way
Which brought us hither.
ALONSO: I say amen, Gonzalo!
GONZALO: Was Milan thrust from Milan, that his issue
Should become kings of Naples? O rejoice
Beyond a common joy! And set it down
With gold on lasting pillars: in one voyage
Did Claribel her husband find at Tunis,
And Ferdinand, her brother, found a wife
Where he himself was lost; Prospero his dukedom
In a poor isle; and all of ourselves,
When no man was his own.†
ALONSO: *[to Ferdinand and Miranda]* Give me your hands.
Let grief and sorrow still embrace his heart
That doth not wish you joy!
GONZALO: Be it so! Amen!

[Re-enter Ariel, with the Master and Boatswain amazedly following]

O look, sir, look, sir! Here is more of us!
I prophesied if a gallows were on land
This fellow could not drown. *[to the Boatswain]* Now, blasphemy,[37]
That swear'st grace o'erboard: not an oath on shore?
Hast thou no mouth by land? What is the news?
BOATS: The best news is that we have safely found
Our King and company; the next, our ship,
Which but three glasses[38] since we gave out[39] split,
Is tight and yare[40] and bravely rigged as when
We first put out to sea.
ARIEL: *[aside to Prospero]* Sir, all this service
Have I done since I went.
PROSP: *[aside to Ariel]* My tricksy spirit!
ALONSO: These are not natural events; they strengthen
From strange to stranger. Say, how came you hither?
BOATS: If I did think, sir, I were well awake

[34] *Miranda*

[35] *sorrow*

[36] *marked out*

[37] *blasphemer*

[38] *hourglasses*

[39] *declared*

[40] *sound and ready to sail*

I'd strive to tell you. We were dead of sleep,
And—how we know not—all clapped under hatches,
Where but even now, with strange and several noises
Of roaring, shrieking, howling, jingling chains,
And more diversity of sounds, all horrible,
We were awaked; straightaway at liberty;
Where we, in all her trim, freshly beheld
Our royal, good and gallant ship, our Master:
Cap'ring to eye[41]here. On a trice, so please you,
Even in a dream, were we divided from them,†
And were brought moping[42] hither.

Ariel: *[aside to Prospero]* Was't well done?

Prosp: *[aside to Ariel]* Bravely, my diligence. Thou shalt be free.

Alonso: This is as strange a maze as e'er men trod,
And there is in this business more than nature
Was ever conduct of. Some oracle
Must rectify our knowledge.

Prosp: Sir, my liege,
Do not infest your mind with beating on[43]
The strangeness of this business. At picked leisure
Which shall be shortly, single[44] I'll resolve you,
Which to you shall seem probable,[45] of every
These happen'd accidents;[46] till when be cheerful
And think of each thing well.
[aside to Ariel] Come hither, spirit.
Set Caliban and his companions free.
Untie the spell. *[Exit Ariel]*
[to Alonso] How fares my gracious sir?
There are yet missing of your company
Some few odd lads that you remember not.

[Re-enter Ariel, driving in Caliban, Stephano, and Trinculo, in their stolen apparel]

Steph: Every man shift for all the rest, and let no man take care for himself; for all is but fortune. Coragio,† bully-monster, coragio!

Trinc: If these[47] be true spies which I wear in my head, here's a goodly sight.

Caliban: O Setebos, these be brave spirits indeed!
How fine my master is! I am afraid
He will chastise me.

Sebastian: Ha, ha!

[41] *Dancing to see*

[42] *dazed*

[43] *repeated worry*

[44] *in private*

[45] *plausible*

[46] *incidents*

[47] *these eyes*

What things are these, my lord Antonio?
Will money buy 'em?

ANTONIO: Very like; one of them
Is a plain fish, and no doubt marketable.

PROSP: Mark but the badges[48] of these men, my lords,
Then say if they be true. This misshapen knave,
His mother was a witch, and one so strong
That could control the moon, make flows and ebbs,
And deal in her command without her power.
These three have robbed me, and this demi-devil,
For he's a bastard one, had plotted with them
To take my life. Two of these fellows you
Must know and own. This thing of darkness I
Acknowledge mine.

CALIBAN: I shall be pinched to death.

ALONSO: Is not this Stephano, my drunken butler?

SEBASTIAN: He is drunk now. Where had he wine?

ALONSO: And Trinculo is reeling ripe. Where should they
Find this grand liquor that hath gilded 'em?[49]
[to Trinculo] How camest thou in this pickle?

TRINC: I have been in such a pickle since I saw you last that, I fear me, will never out of my bones. I shall not fear fly-blowing.†

SEBASTIAN: Why, how now, Stephano?

STEPH: O, touch me not! I am not Stephano, but a cramp.

PROSP: You'd be king o'the isle, sirrah?

STEPH: I should have been a sore[50] one then.

ALONSO: *[pointing to Caliban]* This is a strange thing as e'er I look'd on.

PROSP: He is as disproportioned in his manners
As in his shape. *[to Caliban]* Go, sirrah, to my cell.
Take with you your companions. As you look
To have my pardon, trim[51] it handsomely.

CALIBAN: Ay, that I will; and I'll be wise hereafter,
And seek for grace. What a thrice-double ass
Was I to take this drunkard for a god,
And worship this dull fool!

PROSP: Go to, away! *[Exit Caliban]*

ALONSO: *[to Stephano and Trinculo]* Hence, and bestow your luggage where you found it.

SEBASTIAN: Or stole it, rather.

[Exeunt Stephano and Trinculo]

[48] *uniforms, livery*

[49] *made them drunk*

[50] *pained*

[51] *decorate*

PROSP: *[to Alonso]* Sir, I invite your highness and your train
To my poor cell, where you shall take your rest
For this one night; which, part of it, I'll waste
With such discourse as I not doubt shall make it
Go quick away: the story of my life
And the particular accidents gone by
Since I came to this isle. And in the morn
I'll bring you to your ship, and so to Naples,
Where I have hope to see the nuptial
Of these our dear-belovèd solemnized;
And thence retire me to my Milan, where
Every third thought shall be my grave.

ALONSO: I long
To hear the story of your life, which must
Take the ear strangely.

PROSP: I'll deliver all,
And promise you calm seas, auspicious gales
And sail so expeditious that shall catch
Your royal fleet far off. *[aside to Ariel]* My Ariel, chick,
That is thy charge. Then to the elements
Be free, and fare thou well! *[Exit Ariel]*
Please you, draw near.

[Exeunt all but Prospero]

EPILOGUE

Now my charms are all o'erthrown,
And what strength I have's mine own,
Which is most faint. Now, 'tis true
I must be here confined by you
Or sent to Naples. Let me not,
Since I have my dukedom got,
And pardoned the deceiver, dwell
In this bare island[1] by your spell;
But release me from my bands[2]
With the help of your good hands:[3]
Gentle breath[4] of yours my sails
Must fill, or else my project fails,
Which was to please. Now I want[5]
Spirits to enforce, art to enchant,
And my ending is despair,
Unless I be relieved by prayer,
Which pierces so, that it assaults
Mercy itself, and frees all faults.
As you from crimes would pardoned be,
Let your indulgence[6] set me free.†

[1] *(the stage)*

[2] *shackles*

[3] *applause*

[4] *Positive comments*

[5] *lack*

[6] *approval*

Glossary

<u>Act I: Scene I</u>

"Take in the topsail." – Taking in the topsail reduces the sail's surface area and decreases the wind's ability to push the ship closer to the island.

"Blow...room enough!" – There are two possibilities in interpreting this use of direct address: One is that the Boatswain is speaking directly to the storm, telling it to be as forceful as it can, so long as there is ample room for the ship to maneuver and take the powerful blows of the storm without hitting any reefs or rocks. The other is that the Boatswain is simply telling a mariner to blow on the whistle as loudly as possible.

"What cares...name of king?" – *Roarers* is a term the Boatswain uses in reference to the passengers; however, the term also refers to the rough, stormy waves, in which case it would be an example of personification.

counsellor – Gonzalo is a member of the king's council, but this title also refers to someone who persuades or advises.

"...no drowning mark...perfect gallows." – A birthmark in a specific position was believed to predict a person's death through drowning. A well-known proverb in Shakespeare's time was, "He that is born to be hanged will never be drowned."

"Make the rope...little advantage." – referring to an anchor cable, even though their anchor is of little help in a fierce thunderstorm

"Down...topmast!" – Lowering the topmast decreases the top weight of the ship and makes it more stable.

"Bring her...main-course." – The men want to attempt sailing the ship at an angle into the wind. With this technique, they are hoping that the ship will be pushed away from the island.

"I'll warrant...drowning..." – Gonzalo guarantees the Boatswain will not drown.

"Set her two courses!" – This command refers to setting the foresail and the mainsail, which will help in keeping the ship as close to the wind as possible.

"...lay her off!" – "...get the ship out to sea!"

"...must our mouths be cold?" – A well-known proverb, "to be cold in the mouth" meant "to be dead"; however, other critics interpret the lines to suggest that the mariners warm their cold mouths with liquor.

"The washing of ten tides!" – Antonio is alluding to the punishment for pirates, which was to be hanged during low tide and left until three tides had passed.

"...long heath,...furze anything." – Gonzalo is referring to various shrubs that are all hardy enough to flourish even in poor soil. He would rather be on land, even land barely able to sustain life, than at sea.

<u>Act I: Scene II</u>

pitch – Although *pitch* refers to tar, Miranda is referring specifically to its odor and blackness.

blessèd – Miranda is suggesting Divine intervention.

"transported / And rapt" – Prospero is speaking of being literally carried away to the island, as well as being completely consumed in his studies of sorcery.

creatures – Prospero is referring to those individuals whose positions had been 'created' for them.

"changed 'em...formed 'em..." – having changed the responsibilities of those positions or created new ones

"...the key...what tune..." – Using the metaphor of musical notation allows Prospero to illustrate exactly how much control Antonio possessed. Having the "key" gives Antonio the power to do as he pleases, just as a musician controls the instrument he plays.

"Like a good parent..." – a common conversational phrase: "Good parents breed bad children," like the proverbial, "Great men's sons seldom do well"

"...like one...own lie,..." – like someone who lies so much he or she begins to believe the lies as truth

"To have...play'd it for,..." – Prospero is explaining Antonio's work ethic. According to Prospero, Antonio was unable to separate ("no screen") business ("this part he played") and pleasure ("him he play'd it for").

"...and bend...ignoble stooping." – a reference to Antonio's making Milan, the once independent state, a possession of Naples.

"Good wombs...bad sons." – Miranda interprets Prospero's ill feelings and verbal attacks on Antonio as accusations toward his mother's having committed adultery.

"A rotten carcass of a butt..." – *Carcass* refers to a dilapidated base of a ship, and *butt*, which literally refers to a barrel, is used as another term for *boat*.

"...to sigh...loving wrong." – Prospero is explaining how the winds responded to their cries and blew them farther out to sea.

"burden groaned" – This phrase implies giving birth.

Fortune – personified to emphasize the inexplicable force that was believed to control a person's destiny

"auspicious star" – Prospero, and many others of his day, believed that the stars and other celestial bodies had the power to influence people and events.

"burn in many places" – a reference to "St. Elmo's fire," which is caused by an electrical discharge during a thunderstorm. The discharge would frequently occur at the tips of boat masts. This phenomenon, named by Erasmus of Formia, usually appeared as a bluish-white glow, and, therefore, was often confused for fire.

Jove's lightning – Jove (Jupiter) was the king of the gods in Roman mythology; he used thunderbolts, which the Roman's believed to be a sign of condemnation.

sulphurous – After a lightning bolt strikes, there is the smell of sulfur in the air.

Neptune – (Poseidon) the god of the seas

"sustaining garments" – The mariners were kept afloat by their clothing, which may have been caused by the magic Prospero cast. The use of the word *sustaining* suggests "life-giving" or "life-preserving."

"His arms in this sad knot." – Arms folded across the chest suggest grief, sorrow, or melancholy.

"…for one thing…take her life." – Sycorax was not condemned to death because she was pregnant at the time.

"…got by the devil…dam,…" – Prospero's insult goes much deeper; he implies that the devil mated with Caliban's mother.

"As wicked dew…unwholesome fen…" – Dew was a common ingredient in magic potions (used by both Prospero and Sycorax). In addition, ravens were linked with witchcraft. Interestingly, the Latin word for *raven* is *corax*, which is clearly represented in the name Sycorax.

"…south-west blow…all o'er!" – Winds from the South were thought to bring sickness.

"As thick as honeycomb…" – The pinches on Caliban will be close together, giving the image of bees' honeycombs.

"…the bigger…the less…" – the sun and the moon, an allusion to Genesis 1:16

Miranda: – There is some discrepancy as to who actually speaks these lines. Many critics attribute this speech to Prospero because they believe it is out of character for Miranda. It is possible, however, that these lines are Miranda's. She is not a typical woman because of the time she has spent isolated from the rest of the world. Miranda had no other female to act as a model for her; instead, being raised by her father, she may have acquired traits uncharacteristic of a woman in her day.

red plague – a plague that inflicts red sores

Hag-seed – the offspring of a hag

Setebos – In accounts from Ferdinand Magellan's travels, Setebos is referred to as an evil god of the Patagonians (natives of Patagonia in southern Argentina).

canker – this can refer to either a canker sore, which is spreading and destructive, or a cankerworm, which is the larva of two different types of moths that destroy fruit trees. In addition, the line has numerous interpretations. Prospero could be stating that grief is like a spreading sore or illness that will ultimately disfigure beautiful things. He could also be explaining how grief is attracted to beauty, similar to how the cankerworm larva is attracted to a rose.

maid – unmarried, as in human (not a goddess or spirit)

"At the first sight…changed eyes." – exchanged glances; fallen in love at first sight

"I fear…some wrong…" – Prospero is confronting Ferdinand because of the lie the heir has told. Ferdinand is assuming that he is now the King of Naples because he believes his father is dead.

"fresh-brook mussels" – Mussels found in freshwater cannot be eaten.

Act II: Scene I

"The masters…the merchant…" – "The owner of a merchant ship and the owner of the cargo."

peace – Sebastian puns Alonso's "peace" for "pease," or porridge (pease porridge).

visitor – Antonio refers to Gonzalo as the person who visits the ill and grieving to offer advice and good will.

"So, you're paid." – Antonio has had his laugh and has, therefore, won his prize.

Temperance – Antonio thinks Temperance is a woman's name.

Dido – the ancient Queen of Carthage, who had a scandalous love affair with Aeneas.

"the miraculous harp" – an allusion to Amphion, whose music helped build the walls of Thebes

Ay – Gonzalo is finally recognizing that Tunis was truly Carthage; in the following line, Antonio comments on how long it took Gonzalo to respond.

"You cram...my sense." – Alonso states that he has been force-fed thoughts and opinions; *stomach* refers to *temper* or *disposition* and *sense* refers to *thought* and *feeling*.

"...that o'er his...bowed..." – *Basis* describes the foot of a cliff that has eroded over time from the surf; therefore, the cliffs appear to be bent over the sea.

"Weighed ...should bow." – *Weighed* has two meanings in this context. The first is literal—the weight on the beam will cause it to bend to one side. The second meaning, *pondered* or *considered*, lends to the metaphor, by implying that Alonso's daughter made a very difficult, or "heavy" decision to disobey her father by marrying without his consent.

"...you rub...the plaster." – Gonzalo is telling Sebastian that his words are hurting Alonso more (making his wounds even more sore), when, instead, Sebastian should be trying to make Alonso feel better. *Plaster* here refers to a soothing balm.

"golden age" – a mythological time, during which Italy was supposedly ruled by the god Saturn; the period was believed to have been without conflict, labor, or injustice, and food grew abundantly, with no need for cultivation.

"flat-long" – the flat or dull side of a sword

"gentlemen of brave mettle" – Literally, *mettle* means *courage* or *bravery*, but Shakespeare is also using *mettle* as a pun for *metal*, suggesting that the men are as strong as a sword.

"a-bat-fowling" – using moonlight to attract, then trap birds, using clubs (*bats*) to bring them down

"...I will not...weakly." – "I refuse to put my sensible judgment at risk so foolishly."

"Trebles thee o'er." – "Make you three times greater."

"Hereditary sloth" – Sebastian, being Alonso's younger brother, believes that he is prevented from obtaining fortune or prosperity; Sebastian attributes his laziness to heredity.

"If you but knew...you mock it..." – "If you could only understand that your mockery reveals your true feelings and shows your desires."

"Ambition cannot...discovery there." – Antonio claims that there is no better or higher goal (*hope*) than the crown.

"...though some cast...my discharge." – Note the theatrical metaphor: *cast; perform an act; prologue.* Also note the apparent paradox expressed in *"what's past is prologue,"* meaning that the past predicts the future.

"...I myself could...deep chat." – Antonio states that he could train a *cough* (a type of bird capable of learning and imitating human speech) to talk as wisely as Gonzalo does.

"If 'twere a kibe,...my bosom." – Remember, Antonio is referring to how he sent his brother Prospero into exile. Sebastian asks if Antonio's conscience had been affected by Prospero's exile. Antonio claims that if the action created a sore or pain (*kibe*) he would have been affected, but because he could not feel God speaking to him, he felt no pain. Antonio firmly believes that God would have inflicted him with pain if he were committing a wrongdoing.

"doing thus" – Antonio acts like he is stabbing Gonzalo.

<u>Act II: Scene II</u>

A noise of thunder heard – Caliban interprets this act of nature as a response to his curse on Prospero.

painted – hung, on a sign, to attract customers and spectators

"make a man" – This phrase has two meanings: The fish could 'make a fortune for a man,' and it also means 'to become a man.'

"a dead Indian" – Trinculo is referring to the popular Native American exhibits on display in London at the time.

"I have...spoon." – There was a proverb that stated, "He should have a long spoon that sups with the devil," indicating that if a person must deal with evil, he or she should stay as far away from the devil as possible.

moon-calf – A popular belief was that the moon could have negative impacts and even detrimental effects on unborn children, resulting in miscarriages or deformities.

Neapolitans – inhabitants or natives of Naples

"turn me about" – Trinculo is so happy to find a member from the ship that he tries to dance with Stephano.

"I will kneel to him." – Caliban thinks Stephano is a god.

"kiss the book" – Stephano is telling Trinculo to confirm the oath by kissing the Bible.

"...thou art made like a goose." – Picture Trinculo with his neck outstretched, drinking from Stephano's bottle; with the bottle as his "beak," Trinculo probably resembles a goose. Because geese were thought of as being foolish and timid, being referred to as a goose might also have been another way to describe giddiness or unsteadiness on one's feet.

"...showed me... bush." – There are two legends from which this reference might have come: In the first, a man was exiled to the moon for either stealing a bundle of kindling or gathering the kindling on the Sabbath Day. The "bush" Caliban refers to would, therefore, be the kindling. The second explanation is based on the fact that to many people in Europe, the man in the moon is carrying a bundle of sticks and a lantern.

"get a new man!" – Caliban is addressing this statement to Prospero.

Act III: Scene I

"...their labour...sets off." – The amount of work expended in something is painless if the action or outcome is enjoyable.

"...such baseness...like executor." – "...such a menial task was never performed by someone so noble."

"When this burns,...wearied you." – Miranda, knowing how hard Ferdinand is working, personifies herself through the wood pile, stating that it will cry once it is burned for making Ferdinand work so hard. "'Twill weep" refers to the wood actually oozing resin (a property commonly found in plants) as it is burned.

"Poor worm...shows it." – Worms were typically thought to carry disease, although calling someone "worm" was also known as a term of endearment. Obviously, Prospero is playing on Ferdinand being "sick" with love, but continues the pun with the word "visitation," which suggests both visiting the sick and receiving a "visit" from the plague.

"Admired Miranda!" – Ferdinand is punning on the meaning of Miranda's name, which is "to be wondered at."

"This wooden slavery..." – Ferdinand alludes to Prospero's mistreatment and using the logs as a symbol for slavery.

flesh-fly – a species of fly known for laying eggs in the flesh of the dead

"here's my hand" – Ferdinand and Miranda were actually married by saying these simple words. In Shakespeare's time, such marriages were typical and considered legitimate, despite there being no witnesses or churches.

Act III: Scene 2

"Stephano: *[to Caliban]* **Tell not me."** – Some sources state that Stephano is speaking to Trinculo, whereas others say Caliban; however, although ambiguous, it seems appropriate that Stephano is speaking to Caliban.

standard-bearer – the person in charge of carrying the banner for a military unit

natural – In this context, *natural* would be interpreted as without intelligence; an idiot.

"the next tree" – referring to the gallows, the structure built for hanging criminals

"this thing" – Caliban may be referring to himself here, but he could also be indicating Trinculo.

"knock a nail into his head" – a biblical allusion to both Judges 4:21 and 5:26

Nobody – refers to an invisible character. *Nobody* has a long history dating from its use in the *Odyssey,* when Odysseus tricked the Cyclops.

Act III: Scene III

lakin – Ladykin; a reference to the Virgin Mary

"Praise in departing" – "Save your praise until the very end."

"...Each putter-out...one" – Travelers would profit from their journeys by purchasing a type of insurance from brokers. The traveler paid the broker a sum prior to departing, which was repaid five-fold if the traveler returned to the broker with proof from the destination.

harpy – a mythological creature with wings of a vulture and the face of a woman

"Ling'ring perdition – slow destruction or ruin

Act IV: Scene I

"I do believe...oracle." – "I'd believe it even if a psychic said otherwise."

"weeds" – Flowers typically (traditionally) adorned the bed of the newlywed couple. Prospero's threat is that weeds will replace the flowers if Ferdinand does not obey.

Hymen – the god of marriage

"...When I shall...chained below." – *Phoebus' steeds* is a reference to the mythological horses that pulled Phoebus' chariot and the sun. With this statement, Ferdinand is expressing his anxiousness for his wedding night. His desire to be along with Miranda is so strong that he feels that his wedding night will never come. Note the personification of night being chained.

Iris – goddess of the rainbow and Juno's messenger

Ceres – goddess of agriculture

Queen o'th' Sky – a reference to Juno, Queen of the heavens and goddess of women

Dis – the mythological King of the Underworld. According to the myth, Venus and Cupid made Dis fall in love with Ceres' daughter Proserpine.

Pathos – a city in Cyprus

Dove-drawn – Venus had a dove-drawn chariot

sparrows – considered to be lustful birds; therefore, they were often associated with Venus

"Spring...harvest!" – Ceres, in Greek mythology, declared that spring should arrive six months following the harvest, which suggests there to be no winter. According to myth, Ceres' neglect for the earth during her search for Proserpine became known as winter.

naiads – mythological river nymphs

"great globe" – Not only is this a reference to the world, it is also an allusion to the Globe Theatre.

dropsy – a disease characterized by an excess of fluid in a person's tissue

"under the line" – This phrase has several interpretations. It could be a saying, such as "below the waist." However, it seems likely that the phrase alludes to the proverb, "Thou hast stricken the ball under the line," which means, "You have cheated."

"line and level" – taken from the expression, "by plumb line and carpenter's level," which means "done precisely, by the rules"

"pass of pate" – *Pass* is a fencing term; *pate* refers to the head; therefore, the phrase implies that 'steal by line and level' is a quick-thinking use of intelligence.

"...put some...fingers..." – To be "lime-fingered" suggests refers to stealing the garments. *Lime* is not the fruit, but a fine white powder made from limestone

pinch-spotted – bruised, from being pinched

"pard or cat o'mountain" – references to leopards; *cat o'mountain* alludes to Jeremiah 13:23: "May a man of Ind change his skin, and the cat of the mountain her spots?" The sentence is also written as "Can the Ethiopian change his skin or the leopard its spots?"

<u>Act V: Scene I</u>

carriage – The word "carriage" refers to a burden or load, which has now been lifted, making it lighter and easier to carry or bear. "Time" therefore, continues to move forward.

"...that relish...as they..." – "who feel the same strong emotion as they do"

ringlets – Mushrooms that sprouted during the night and then were harvested left barren ground or only grass where they had been. When people saw these circular areas, legends and stories claimed dancing fairies formed them.

curfew – It was common practice that a bell was rung at nightfall to announce that spirits would be roaming about the area.

Weak masters – creatures that cannot act independently and require the use of supernatural powers

"But this rough...drown my book." – In this monologue, Prospero admits to all his magical knowledge, but, in the end, realizes his sin and is prepared to give up his necromantic knowledge to be given the chance to return to Naples.

subtilties – illusions; also sweet cakes (subtleties) shaped like castles, temples, beasts, etc.

"***Here...playing at chess***" – Miranda and Ferdinand playing chess is significant because the entire play is like a game of chess. Prospero's aim throughout has been to capture the king.

"...for a score...fair play." – "...you would fight for twenty kingdoms if I did not accuse you of cheating."

"I am hers." – Alonso is now Miranda's father through marriage.

"When no man was his own." – suggesting a loss of the senses; madness

"Even in a dream...from them,..." – The dream motif runs throughout the play, but becomes more prominent in this final scene. The magic that Prospero has cast throughout the play has been associated with dreams or the act of dreaming. This concept of dream-like occurrences makes Prospero's magic realistic.

Coragio – [Italian] "take courage"

"I shall not fear fly-blowing" – Trinculo is punning on his statement about being in a tough spot—in a pickle. "Fly-blowing" refers to being infested with flies, which he does not have to worry about because he has been "pickled" (preserved).

Epilogue

"Now my charms…set me free." – The use of magic during Shakespeare's day was viewed as real and was feared by many individuals. In *The Tempest,* Shakespeare uses the dream motif and Prospero's desire for redemption as a way for the audience to sympathize with Prospero as a character. His epilogue asks the audience for their forgiveness so he can be set free from his life of evil and magic. He is remorseful for his deeds and desires forgiveness. With the applause from the audience, Prospero (and Shakespeare) have earned the audience's applause and, therefore, their approval.

Vocabulary

Act I: Scene I

blasphemous – verbally abusive; insulting to God

cur – a coward; an undesirable dog (this insult works in conjunction with Sebastian's previous insult when he refers to the Boatswain as an "incharitable dog.")

furlongs – measures of distance; a *furlong* is one-eighth of a mile

insolent – arrogant

mar – to damage; spoil

pox – a disease (usually smallpox)

whoreson – a son of a whore

Act I: Scene II

advocate – a supporter

allay – to reduce, alleviate

apparition – a supernatural appearance

auspicious – prosperous

besiege – to surround

bowsprit – a wooden pole that extends forward from the front of a ship that sails are secured to

brine – seawater; the ocean

brine-pits – salt springs

chide – to scold, reprimand

cloven – split

confer – to give, bestow

coronet – a crown of lesser value, showing the wearer's inferiority to the king

correspondent – obedient, respectful, compliant

direful – devastating, tragic

fortitude – mental strength that provides courage to endure adversity

gallant – a well-dressed, dignified man; a fine gentleman

gape – to open

hatches – small doors within the ship

homage – acknowledgement of loyalty

ignoble – not one of nobility; common

inveterate – firmly, officially

knell – the sound of a bell rung for a funeral

levied – gathered

malice – a desire to harm others; here the form of direct address shows Caliban's true nature

malignant – evil, spiteful

manacle – to restrain; chain

Neapolitan – a native or one who lives in Naples

passion – grief, suffering
perfidious – deceitful, traitorous
pitch – tar
precursors – predecessors; someone or something that indicates or announces an event or action that is to come
prescience – foresight; knowing something will happen before it occurs
quaint – ingenious, skillful; curious in appearance; elegant
rend – to split into pieces in anger; tear away
reputed – considered (referring to reputation)
revenue – income, profits
rift – a narrow opening
stick – Prospero's magician's wand
surety – guarantee; hostage
temporal – temporary. Interestingly, *temporal* refers to the skull, which can be loosely interpreted as *knowledge* or *intelligence*, considering Prospero is speaking of his library.
trident – a three-pronged spear
twain – two
unbowed – stiff; not controlled or oppressed; independent
unmitigable – not relievable
urchins – hedgehogs; Prospero is indicating that his spirits will be disguised as hedgehogs
usurp – to take or assume falsely
vast – an expansive area
verdure – lushness; green foliage
vouchsafe – to grant, allow
ward – a defensive stance
whelp – a child
zenith – the highest point; in this context, Prospero is speaking of his own good fortune.

Act II: Scene I

Beseech – to ask
contentious – quarrelsome, combative
cubit – a measure of distance; it was originally determined by the length of a person's forearm, which resulted in varying measurements. A cubit usually measured between 18 and 22 inches.
docks – hardy weed-like herbs that were said to remedy the stings from the nettle plants
doublet – a jacket
enmity – hatred
importuned – begged, pleaded

kibe – a sore on the heel of a foot; chilblain
mallows – weeds; the roots excrete a type of ointment that also soothe the "nettle stings."
nettle-seed – a type of plant with leaves that irritate the skin
paragon – a perfect example; perfection
plantation – the power to colonize
prate b– to talk senselessly
repose – a rest, period of relaxation; sleep
sloth – laziness
succession – the ability to inherit property
supplant – to remove

Act II: Scene 2
boatswain – a ship officer in charge of the rigging, anchors, and crew members
bombard – an early cannon; also a leather jug used for drinking liquor, which may have resembled a cannon
chaps – lips
credulous – gullible, easy to believe
dregs – residue (usually referring to wine)
filberts – hazelnuts
firebrand – a piece of burning wood
marmoset – a small monkey
mire – a swamp
scurvy – horrible
sooth – truth

Act III: Scene I
baseness – low, common; not decent
crabbed – crabby, morose
dower – dowry; money or property given to the groom from the bride's family before marriage
injunction – an order, command
invert – to turn upside down
odious – repulsive
precepts – orders, instructions
sinews – ligaments, tendons

Act III: Scene II
brine – seawater
debauched – evil, mean
dowl – a feather
drollery – a puppet show

flout – to show hatred or scorn
jocund – lighthearted
pied – multicolored
plume – plumage; elaborate dress; the use of feathers in clothing
pox – a mild curse; related to smallpox
sack – wine
scout – to reject with hatred; to mock
tabor – a small drum
viceroys – governors
vigilance – watchfulness

Act IV: Scene I
abstemious – sparing, restricted; stingy
austerely – sternly, severely
betrims – covered with flowers
bosky – covered with thickets and shrubs
broom-groves – thickets filled with broom bushes (shrubs with yellow flowers)
cleave – to stick to; to be faithful to
furzes – thorny shrubs
garners – storage buildings for grain
hogshead – a large barrel
infirmity – weakness, frailty
lass-lorn – abandoned by the girl he pursued
marred – damaged, destroyed
pionèd – dug, excavated
revels – merrymaking
saffron – orange-yellow in color
sanctimonious – holy
sedged – referring to grass-like plants; reeds
smote – past tense of *smite*; to hit
vetches – pea-like plants
vexations – annoyances, irritations
wetting – "my becoming wet"

Act V: Scene I
abjure – to give up
auspicious – good, favorable
pentinent – feeling remorse
rapier – a sword

Epilogue
—